connecting mathematical ideas

connecting mathematical ideas

Middle School Video Cases to Support Teaching and Learning

Jo Boaler
Cathy Humphreys

Foreword by
Deborah Loewenberg Ball

HEINEMANN
Portsmouth, NH

Heinemann

361 Hanover Street
Portsmouth, NH 03801–3912
www.heinemann.com

Offices and agents throughout the world

The authors and Heinemann acknowledge the support of the Noyce Foundation in developing the video cases. All video footage is used by permission of the Noyce Foundation.

Library of Congress Cataloging-in-Publication Data
Boaler, Jo, 1964–
  Connecting mathematical ideas : middle school video cases to support teaching and learning / Jo Boaler and Cathy Humphreys.
    p. cm.
  Includes bibliographical references.
  ISBN 0-325-00670-9
  1. Mathematics—Study and teaching (Middle school)—Audio-visual aids.
2. Mathematics—Programmed instruction.   I. Humphreys, Cathy.   II. Title.

  QA20 .P7B63 2005
  510' .71'2—dc22   2004027856

Editor: Victoria Merecki
Production: Lynne Costa
Cover design: Catherine Hawkes, Cat & Mouse
Typesetter: Argosy
Manufacturing: Steve Bernier

Printed in the United States of America on acid-free paper
13 12 11 10 09 VP 6 7 8 9 10

Contents

Foreword

Teaching is a basic human activity. Parents, friends, nurses, salespeople, and taxi drivers all teach others. They explain, they help others do things, they demonstrate, and they guide. Teaching is so commonplace that the need—in order to do it well for special skills, knowledge, and sensibilities—is often not appreciated. Teaching often seems natural, something we do in the course of our everyday efforts to help others.

If we all do it in the course of everyday life, then what is there to see or to say about teaching? That it seems so natural serves to make teaching appear obvious, hardly worthy of study, discussion, and refinement.

Yet anyone who has tried to help young people learn mathematics appreciates that the ability to teach math well is far from obvious. Moreover, anyone who has struggled to learn mathematics from a teacher who could not communicate or connect the content to the students realizes that teaching math well is far from a natural act. Helping someone else learn requires a kind of scrutiny of the mathematical ideas different from learning them oneself.

This scrutiny of ideas is neither natural nor commonplace. What do letters mean in an algebraic formula? Why is 1 not considered a prime number? Why are two 10 percent reductions not the same as one 20 percent reduction—and what exactly is the difference between the two? What does $3\frac{1}{2} \div \frac{3}{4}$ *mean*? Is it three-quarters of three and a half? What is a clear representation that shows what $3\frac{1}{2} \div \frac{3}{4}$ actually signifies? Why isn't $\frac{0}{0} = 1$? Or 0?

Teachers who simply know how to do math well themselves will sometimes also be good teachers. They can use their own understanding to try to illuminate others'. But as often as not, learners ask questions. They make sense of the ideas, but it is a different sense than that intended by their teacher. They make errors, they forget, they confound one idea with another. And, hence, the mathematical work of the teacher escalates. Figuring out what someone else is thinking is harder than simply giving an answer. Giving an explanation that someone else can follow is harder than explaining something to yourself. Sequencing a series of examples so that the work gradually becomes more challenging requires a level of mathematically sensitive design that goes well beyond offering a handful of illustrations. And, as Jo Boaler and Cathy Humphreys show us vividly in this book and the accompanying CDs, questioning is a finely composed piece of mathematical work tuned to particular learners. For these and other central and recurrent tasks of teaching, teachers need to know and use mathematics in specialized ways.

Teachers use specialized knowledge of mathematics together with knowledge of students to calibrate the pace and structure of the content as it unfolds. They talk, they ask students to talk, and they listen. The unusual set of case materials presented here combines video extracts from a seventh-grade class with written commentaries by both the classroom teacher and a university teacher and researcher. The video extracts make vividly apparent the dexterity required in skillful teaching. The commentaries make available language with which to describe and discuss the practice. Both outsider insight and insider perspectives are articulated.

Cathy Humphreys is an experienced middle school teacher who has deliberately worked on the challenges of teaching mathematics in ways that allow students to experience math's wonder, interest, and power. Here she provides a window into the particularities of pedagogical reasoning. She gives insight into students and the typical difficulties they face. She offers a pedagogical perspective on the mathematics discussed. Her experience tells her that improved content standards alone cannot improve student learning. She knows that the details of her instructional decisions and moves are what shape the actual curriculum. The video extracts offer opportunities to study these moves; her detailed commentaries offer opportunities to learn about the pedagogical reasoning that underlay those moves.

For example, her launch of the Border Problem (see Chapter 2) provides an intricate case of teaching practice. That problems require carefully chosen wording, and that their numeric and geometric details matter, is one element of pedagogical design. That their initiation into classroom work requires similarly careful development is another. Cathy chose to tell her students to figure out the number of unit tiles in the border "without talking, without writing, and without counting one by one." Why all these constraints? In her reflection, Cathy carefully explains: She wanted the students' work to produce a wide variety of methods, she wanted the students to find methods that could generalize, and she knew that approaching the problem with these constraints would yield rich work that she could use for the whole-group discussion. Studying her design and the reasons that underlie it offers the opportunity to work inside the boundary that usually keeps teaching practice invisible. Bringing light to the details of practice enables a special and much-needed kind of professional learning.

The extracts, selected from a year's worth of videotapes, are not special performances, but are samples from real, ongoing practice, with its attendant moments of surprise, struggle, disappointment, and success. Because teaching depends on complex interactions among students, the teacher, and the teacher and students' engagement with the mathematics, it lacks a sure and precise script. Cathy shares with us her analyses, including observations about missteps and decisions that did not bear fruit. In this way, both the thinking and the performance of practice are made available for study.

This book of cases is special because it offers commentaries not only by the professional whose teaching is made available for study but also by a colleague, Jo Boaler, an experienced teacher and a researcher and teacher educator. The bifocal perspective offered through these two professionals' commentaries provides significant support for studying the cases.

For example, Jo's comments on the Border Problem focus us on the role of planning and design in the enactment of problems and students' learning of content. She highlights ways in which Cathy's design was crucial for the nature of the mathematical work afforded by the problem. She notes that Cathy's plan set up the students' work on the problem in a particular way—to precipitate particular methods of counting, to express these algebraically, and to compare the different methods analytically. Boaler points out how different this is from, for instance, a teacher simply extracting all the different methods students develop for counting the border. The nature of what students do on this problem is a function of the teacher's design in the launch and structuring of students' work on the problem.

Jo's comments throughout the collection offer different paths for studying the videos and Cathy's commentaries. For example, Jo identifies research that might be examined in the context of these cases. In the case of the Border Problem, she makes a connection to the work of Stein et al. (2000) on the use of cognitively challenging mathematical tasks in classrooms. These researchers found that as teachers sought to help students with mathematically complex problems, the cognitive demand of the tasks was often reduced. Jo's comments suggest one perspective that could be used to investigate the lesson extracts in this collection—namely, what does the teacher do to manage this recurrent problem in classrooms?

In a profession still so lacking in useful language and tools for its careful study, this set of cases offers resources that can be used in a variety of ways for the disciplined investigation of practice. For example, readers, working individually or in groups, might study the mathematics of the problems portrayed across the cases. They might do the problems themselves, study Cathy's commentaries on her framing and goals, and then investigate closely how the mathematical ideas and purposes develop in the course of the lessons. Readers might develop similar problems and compare their mathematical possibilities. They might examine textbooks to see how core ideas connected to these problems are treated in different curriculum materials, and they might examine state frameworks to learn where and how the related ideas and skills appear, and with what emphasis.

Other sorts of uses focus more squarely on the pedagogy of the mathematical ideas. How do these problems offer students opportunities to study the mathematical ideas, and how do Cathy's moves and decisions shape those learning opportunities? How does Cathy manage certain endemic challenges of teaching— for instance, covering curriculum and pacing, integrating skill development with understanding and attending to diversity? Groups might seek to identify particular moves that Cathy makes and discuss their purpose and effect, as well as what their enactment seems to require. Individual practitioners might experiment with some of the approaches or moves that Cathy makes and discuss what happens in their own classes.

These materials would also be useful to provide common ground for discussing mathematics teaching and learning across communities. For example, a video excerpt might be used as the basis for a school board discussion, at a parent meeting, or to support grounded conversation between university faculty and school professionals.

Jo Boaler and Cathy Humphreys have assembled a rich resource for the study of practice, with useful tools to support a variety of uses. The improvement of students' opportunities to learn mathematics depends fundamentally on teachers' skill and knowledge. No curriculum or framework is self-enacting, no students self-teaching. Moreover, teachers are often expected to teach mathematical topics and skills in ways substantially different from the ways in which they themselves learned that content. Many teachers, for example, learned functions entirely in the context of traditional high school algebra courses, where the skill of graphing equations overpowered the conceptual and representational issues. Hence, if students' learning is to improve, teachers' professional learning opportunities are key.

Teaching mathematics demands a level of knowledge, skill, thoughtfulness, and fluency that is too often invisible. When we see good teachers, we are reduced to commenting on their "natural talent," as though teaching cannot be learned. This collection offers an antidote to this discouraging perspective on the practice of teaching. For teachers to teach mathematics effectively, they need opportunities to learn mathematics for teaching, and to learn to use mathematics in their work. They need opportunities to examine closely the pedagogical moves and considerations that constitute high-quality practice. These cases provide practice-based resources for study and analysis. The authors' experience and expertise with practice show in the design of this special collection. The materials provide resources that can help make the interior of practice available for scrutiny and study and thus turn teaching from a natural, but rare, talent to a professional practice that can be studied, learned, and—individually and collectively—improved.

Deborah Loewenberg Ball
University of Michigan

Acknowledgments

Many people have contributed in important ways to the development of this book and the work upon which it is based. The initial video project was made possible by the support of David Foster and the Noyce Foundation, and we are very grateful to them. Kim Austin contributed in significant ways to the development of the cases and Kim Powell to the collection of multimedia extracts. As we worked on our book, we were helped immeasurably by the insights of various members of Jo's mathematics research team at Stanford—Karin Brodie, Nikki Cleare, Jennifer DiBrenza, Nick Fiori, Melissa Gresalfi, Tesha Sengupta, Emily Shahan, Megan Staples, and Toby White. Sally Keyes and Joan Carlson also made important contributions to the ideas expressed. The students at Graham Middle School gave life to our project; without them the cases would not have been possible. Finally, the unwavering support of our partners, Bob Humphreys and Colin Haysman, played an essential role and is deeply appreciated.

—*Cathy & Jo*

Introduction

Jo Boaler

When I was ten years old I had what I can only describe as a mysti-
cal experience. It came during a math class. We were learning about
circles, and to his eternal credit our teacher, Mr. Marshall, let us
discover for ourselves the secret image of this unique shape: the num-
ber known as pi. Almost everything you want to say about circles
can be said in terms of pi, and it seemed to me in my childhood inno-
cence that a great treasure of the universe had just been revealed.
Everywhere I looked I saw circles, and at the heart of every one of
them was this mysterious number. It was in the shape of the sun and
the moon and the earth; in mushrooms, sunflowers, oranges, and
pearls; in wheels, clock faces, crockery, and telephone dials. All of
these things were united by pi, yet it transcended them all. I was
enchanted. It was as if someone had lifted a veil and shown me a
glimpse of a marvelous realm beyond the one I experienced with my
senses. From that day on I knew I wanted to know more about the
mathematical secrets hidden in the world around me.

MARGARET WERTHEIM (1997, P3–4)

There are many reasons that I love this quote. Most significantly, it reminds me of
the wonder of childhood—the excitement that children experience when they
learn new ideas that help them make sense of the world around them. Wertheim
was encouraged to see mathematics as an explanatory power that could be used to
interpret patterns in the world, and this experience helped her see new connections. "A marvelous realm beyond the one I experienced with my own senses" is a
lovely description of mathematics, alluding to the hidden power of the subject—
the ability to make connections where there are seemingly none. Pi, as Wertheim
saw it, was particularly important because it "united" all of the circles she saw. She

1

was encouraged to understand pi and her understanding helped her see the world differently. This quote also prompts an inevitable question: Why are school mathematics classrooms not full of similar acts of sense making, connections, and wonder? It seems that the essential components are there—natural childhood curiosity and a subject that is all about relationships, connections, and explanatory power. But instead of creating mathematics students who are curious and excited we more frequently produce students who regard mathematics as drudgery, a vast collection of standard methods that have to be memorized and regurgitated (Schoenfeld 1988; Boaler 1997, 2002b). In this book and the accompanying classroom CDs, you will see students engaged in a very different endeavor as they embark on a yearlong journey of sense making, inquiry, and wonder.

This book is intended as a guiding companion to eight cases of teaching and an accompanying set of student interviews. The cases come from a year-long project videotaping two seventh-grade mathematics classes. The Noyce Foundation funded researchers at Stanford University to film classes taught by Cathy Humphreys throughout one school year. Many professional videos of teachers offer snapshots of lessons filmed on a specially prepared day, in which everything appears to run smoothly. In this project we filmed every day for an entire year, capturing everything and anything that happened. The lesson extracts we present reveal the unpredictability and complexity of classroom life. Where the cases have been edited to remove certain extracts, the purpose has been to highlight the more salient moments and make the extracts relatively succinct.

In the chapter that accompanies each case, Cathy writes about her aims and goals for each lesson as well as her reflections on the events that transpired. Our intention is that viewers of each case will read Cathy's notes about designing the lesson before they watch the case, then watch the case of teaching, and then return to the book to read Cathy's reflections. In each of the chapters I also include my thoughts on points of particular interest, written as a "case commentary" (J. Shulman 1992, 131). Together we frame the case for readers, giving additional ideas and information that we hope will be of interest. We have also included on the CDs some discussion questions that we hope will be a source of reflection for those watching the cases alone and a source of discussion for those watching the cases with others.

The different cases may be summarized as follows:

Chapter 2: Building on Student Ideas—The teacher introduces the students to algebra; the class examines and compares different student methods and makes connections between algebra and geometry.

Chapter 3: Building Understanding of Algebraic Representation—The teacher and students work on forming algebraic expressions and understanding variables. They also talk about functional dependency.

Chapter 4: Defending Reasonableness—The class considers discussing wrong answers, convincing others, representing ideas, and reasoning.
Chapter 5: Introducing the Notion of Proof—The class begins a discussion about convincing and proving.
Chapter 6: Continuing Our Discussion of Proof—The class continues its discussion of proof and algebraic equivalence.
Chapter 7: Class Participation—Classmates share their feelings on talking publicly and different methods of eliciting participation.
Chapter 8: Volume of Prisms and Cylinders—The teacher asks students to connect the volume of rectangular prisms to the volume of cylinders and work on visualizing volumes.
Chapter 9: Surface Area—The class works on deriving a formula for the surface area of a cylinder.

On CD 2, we also include two interviews with students who were involved in the class discussions. In interview 1 (Reflections on Fraction Discussion) the students reflect on the fraction discussion and other aspects of Cathy's teaching. In interview 2 (Reflections on Teaching) a different set of students considers the teaching more generally.

We chose to title this book *Connecting Mathematical Ideas* to reflect two forms of connection making featured in the cases. In all of the teaching extracts, you will see connections being encouraged between students' ideas and between student and teacher ideas, as Cathy works to support small-group and whole-class discussions. You will also see connections between areas of mathematics as Cathy encourages reflection on the links between different mathematical ideas, between different mathematical representations, and between different domains such as algebra and geometry.

Our goal in collaborating on this project—Cathy, a middle school mathematics teacher with more than twenty-five years of teaching experience, and myself, a former teacher in England and now a university teacher and researcher in the States—was to provide a landscape of teaching and learning interactions that others could use to explore their own thoughts and questions about teaching. Cases of teaching provide a special opportunity for teachers to learn and grow, not by communicating answers or presenting model teaching, but by prompting *questions*, as Lee Shulman has written: "the materials must be of sufficient complexity, admit enough alternate readings, invite enough enthusiastic disagreements and contrary views to be worth the energetic investments in dialogue of a learning community" (1992, 20). In the different lesson extracts that are the focus of the cases, we see a teacher encouraging her students to grapple with complex mathematical ideas, to connect what they are learning to what they know, and to understand mathematics and the connections it embodies. By engaging in different inquiries, stu-

range of insights on relationships and structures. Student thinking and sense making are at the heart of each case, as we see students wrestle with new ideas and conceptions of themselves, of mathematics, and ultimately, of their world. In each case readers will see a broad range of pedagogical practices that engage, enrich, and enhance the students' experiences with mathematics.

Over recent years there has been recognition that the effectiveness of any teaching and learning situation will depend upon the actual students involved, the particular curriculum materials used, and the myriad of decisions that teachers make as they support student learning. In short, "teaching occurs in particulars" (Ball and Cohen 1999, 10). Teachers have traditionally been offered general principles and strategies about education, abstracted from the particulars of specific teaching and learning events. Such abstract knowledge can, in certain circumstances, be extremely powerful, but it leaves to teachers the task of translating it into practical action in their own classrooms (Schwab 1969; Bolster 1983). An exciting development of recent years is the awareness that actual records of teaching and learning—videos of classrooms, teacher reflections, student work, and other materials—are extremely powerful sites for learning (Ball and Cohen, 1999; Lampert 2001). Teachers and researchers are finding that analyses grounded in actual practice allow a kind of awareness and learning that has not previously been possible. We hope our cases of teaching will provide such an example of practice and that the details that are portrayed will serve as sites for both inquiry and learning. Just as the students in the cases are learning through their mathematical inquiries, we hope that such inquiries may serve as a source for teacher learning as teachers pose their own questions about the interactions they see.

It is impossible for teachers to start their careers knowing everything they need to know about the ways to act in different situations with different students. New curriculum materials are published daily, initiatives emerge from districts and schools that require different work of teachers, technological advances provide new opportunities for the representation and learning of mathematical ideas. But more important than all of the new initiatives and materials is the unique nature of student thinking. In every interaction in which a teacher engages, she is faced with a new set of student ideas, conceptions, and beliefs. As teachers have conversations with students, probing their thinking and offering new challenges, they have to make important decisions in the moment. The complexity of a teacher's work is demonstrated well by the demands faced when questioning a student. Consider how complicated the act of teacher questioning really is: First, the teacher needs to hear what the student has to say, understand his reasoning, and locate his ideas in the broader mathematical terrain. Then the teacher has to consider what the student is capable of and willing to do as well as consider what is a mathematically productive direction for the student (and the class). Then the teacher has to process all of this information and pose a good question, one that is accessible, challenging, and useful. All of this thinking has to take place in an instant, in the midst of an interaction that involves a class full of students. Questioning students is extremely cognitively demanding. It is no wonder that subject knowledge is so critical to good teaching and that teachers need a particular kind of highly specialized knowledge. In a seminal piece of work, Lee Shulman identified the specialized knowledge that teachers need and named it *pedagogical content knowledge* (1986, 9). Shulman described this knowledge as "the blending of content and pedagogy into an understanding of how particular topics, problems or issues are organized, represented, and adapted to the diverse interests and abilities of learners, and presented for instruction" (1987, 8). But where do teachers learn such rich and specialized knowledge? Ball and Bass (2000) point out that a mathematics teacher needs a particular kind of knowledge that would not be held by a mathematician nor by a social studies teacher. High-level courses in mathematics focus on content, which is helpful but doesn't comprise this special constellation of ideas (Ball and Bass 2000). University methods classes and professional development sessions often focus upon pedagogy (Ball and Cohen 1999). But Shulman, Ball, and others have argued that it is the combination of content and pedagogy that is so important for teaching. In presenting a series of teacher cases, we hope to provide a venue for teachers to consider student ideas, productive questions, teacher moves, and other aspects of the work of teaching that help enhance pedagogical content knowledge.

Chapter 1

Opening the Door to My Classroom

Cathy Humphreys

After all, what one believes about teaching and learning is compli-
cated, large-scale, hard-to-define, and close to the soul.

DUCKWORTH (1987a, 130)

My Teaching Journey

I started my career as a fourth-grade teacher with no particular love of math. I had liked math in school, though, especially the systematic precision of algebra and the step-by-step logic of geometry. But Algebra II was more elusive, and I soon lost interest. It was my last high school mathematics course. One dreary Math for Elementary School Teachers course was the only other math class I took before entering the classroom as a teacher.

I began teaching as I had been taught. I thought math was arithmetic, that teaching math was showing methods, and that learning math meant carefully following procedures. I was enthusiastic and positive; I tried to convey to my students the idea that math was understandable and that they all could be successful. I was evaluated as an exceptional teacher. But, although I felt good about my instruction most of the time, some timely experiences set me on a new path.

The first experience was like being doused with a bucket of cold water. I changed grade levels, from sixth to seventh grade, and by chance ended up with many of the students I had taught the year before. When I gave a beginning-of-the-year arithmetic assessment, I was baffled by how much my students had forgotten. Despite the fact that in sixth grade most of them had "learned" what I had "taught" (I use quotation marks here because I was beginning to wonder if I had taught them anything!), they made the same kinds of errors they had made at the beginning of the previous year—confusing rules for fractions, forgetting rules for

7

decimals, and ending up with wildly unreasonable answers on whole-number computations. More worrisome was their performance on this problem: $\frac{1}{4} \div \frac{1}{4}$. Most of the students multiplied by the reciprocal—some incorrectly—to find the answer! It apparently had never occurred to them to consider this problem holistically and to recognize immediately that any number divided by itself must be one whole. What had gone wrong? Where I had once been so sure about what I had been doing, I now was filled with doubt. I had thought my instruction was really good! I had given clear and careful explanations (and could do so in many different ways), always showing why procedures worked. I had given plenty of guided and independent practice and had been conscientious about collecting and correcting homework. Chapter test results were largely successful. The students thought they were learning; I thought they were, too. Why, then, didn't they remember, only a few months later? It looked like I would need to teach the same thing all over again. What should I do differently? I did not have a clue. One thing was, although hard to admit, crystal clear: my teaching methods had not been successful.

I suspected that I was not the only teacher for whom this was true, but an insightful article later verified just how widespread my experience was. James Hiebert, in "Relationships Between Research and the NCTM Standards," says, "But, presuming that traditional approaches have proven to be successful is ignoring the largest database we have. The evidence indicates that the traditional curriculum and instructional methods in the United States are not serving our students well" (1999, 13). Another absorbing article by Alan Schoenfeld (1988) gave me further insight. Schoenfeld talks about the many students who have mastered procedures without mastering the underlying substance, saying, "Being able to perform the appropriate algorithmic procedures, although important, does not necessarily indicate any depth of understanding" (148). Until then I had unwittingly focused on the mastery of procedures, thinking that this *was* mathematics. I was beginning to realize otherwise.

The next disconcerting event occurred when I administered our new state assessment (the California Assessment Program), which was very different from other state tests I had given. Most of the items were in contexts, and there was a lot of geometry and problem solving. I was baffled; I had spent almost the whole year on arithmetic, which constituted only about 25 percent of this test. It led me to challenge my assumptions about what math *is*—obviously a lot more than arithmetic—and what middle school students should be learning.

Finally, The Math Solution, a professional development course I took at about the same time, provided the catalyst that, together with the other experiences I had just had, made me realize the necessity of changing what and how I taught. During that course, I had a mathematical epiphany as I worked with two other teachers to investigate a function modeled by a growth pattern of Cuisenaire® Rods. In the process of recording the results in a table of values, looking for patterns, writing an equation, and finally graphing the relationship, it dawned on me that there were predictable connections among the graph, the table of values, and the equation of a functional relationship. After working with a number of other growing patterns, I realized that I could visualize a graph from its equation. Was there a constant difference in both the input and output numbers? If so, the line would be straight. I could tell how steep it would be, and I knew where it would cross the y-axis! Suddenly the table of values had come alive for me. I was able to generate expressions for both linear and nonlinear functions, and I tinkered with writing equivalent expressions that matched different ways of visualizing the growth. I remember sitting in the hotel room, sharing my delight with a colleague.

For many people, my discoveries may seem trivial—for some, shockingly so. But for me, as for many of my colleagues, mathematics had always been about following directions. It had not occurred to me that the directions that I had been following (e.g., "Plot the points in the table"; "Find the equation of the line given two points") were rooted in powerful mathematical relationships to which I could gain access in a variety of ways. I learned that I had developed an "instrumental" understanding of algebra (what to do) rather than a "relational" understanding (what to do and *why*) (Skemp 1978). I felt cheated! What else about mathematics had I been missing?

These events launched a personal journey that continues today. How can I help all of my students develop understanding of the important ideas and relationships in mathematics? How can I help them establish the connections among mathematical ideas that have had such a powerful impact on my own learning? What will this mean for *what* I teach? What will it mean for *how* I teach? What does this imply for the mathematics I need to know? All of these questions have meant challenging my deeply held assumptions about what learning mathematics is—and what that implies for its teaching. The video selections you will see, and the writing that accompanies them, reveal my current location in this complex terrain.

About the Videotaping

At the time these lessons took place, I was teaching two periods at Graham Middle School in Mountain View, California. A graduate student from Jo's teacher education program at Stanford University videotaped a lesson from one of my classes almost every day. My students initially were excited and proud to be videotaped, but very soon the camera became another piece of equipment to which they paid little notice. Once every week or two I met with Jo, some of her graduate students, and occasionally other teachers to watch lessons and discuss what we noticed.

This process was not easy for me. Teaching as a profession has been enacted in isolation and shrouded in norms of privacy and individualism, and I am no different than other teachers in this respect. Initially, watching and analyzing my teaching with others was difficult—sometimes downright embarrassing. Even though I know that we must break away from these norms of privacy and make our work transparent if we are to learn about teaching from one another, there is such a personal element to teaching that it took a while for me to gain enough distance from my work to be objective in its analysis. The ability to gain this perspective has been a wonderful result of this project for me.

About the Students and the Curriculum

Graham Middle School has sixth-, seventh-, and eighth-grade students who are placed in two tracks based on their perceived mathematical ability; my classes were from the higher of the two tracks. The students in the video selections are seventh graders from my first- and third-period classes. From September through December I had only one class, which you will see in four of the cases (Chapters 4, 7, 8, and 9). In January I took over a second class for a teacher on maternity leave, and you will meet these students in the remaining four cases.

As sixth graders, these students had completed six units from the *Connected Mathematics Project* (Lappan et al. 1998), supplemented with work from a traditional textbook. The curriculum we were using in seventh grade included sixth- and seventh-grade *CMP* units in addition to one unit I had written, as well as regular problem solving, computation practice, and weekly experiences with numerical reasoning.

Watching the Videos

As teachers, we view teaching with a natural tendency toward lesson repair, which all lessons need to some degree. The video selections you will see, however, were not chosen because they show carefully orchestrated or crafted lessons. All lessons, no matter how ideal, unfold differently in subtle and not so subtle ways with different groups of students; every teacher has experienced lessons that developed perfectly with one group of students while falling flat with another. We chose instead to focus our lens on particularly interesting, unexpected, and sometimes difficult moments that occurred during ordinary lessons. We believed the moments that gave those of us viewing the lessons the most to talk about would offer other professionals the greatest potential for productive scrutiny.

A Theme Emerges

As we assembled our selections, we noticed that, although no common mathematical content united our selections, many of them occurred as students were grappling with making connections among mathematical ideas, representations, or models or with real-world contexts. I have come to believe that this act of building connections and relationships is at the heart of mathematical proficiency. "If curriculum and instruction focus on mathematics as a discipline of connected ideas, students learn to expect mathematical ideas to be related" (NCTM 2000, 275). As students make these connections and develop understanding of these relationships for themselves, the fabric of their mathematical proficiency becomes ever more flexible and sturdy. And as teachers, if we are able to more profoundly connect our mathematical understanding to our growing understandings of how children learn mathematics, the fabric of our own teaching can become stronger. In the words of Jim Greeno, another professor of education at Stanford, "Teachers need to feel as if they can walk around in this terrain, getting from one location to another via a variety of routes" (in Hiebert et al. 1977, 35).

About My Beliefs

To help you understand the context of each video selection, there are sections in each chapter describing the rationale for each of the lessons and portraying what happened in class before the video selection begins. Since the values and beliefs that guide my teaching decisions are more visible in some instances than in others, I will attempt here to articulate some of the beliefs closest to the heart of my teaching.

First, I believe that *learning mathematics* means making sense of mathematical relationships. There are no shortcuts here; no one can do this for another person. Some conventions must be committed to memory and some procedures followed, but everyone must make sense of the relationships for herself. Learning mathematics also means getting better at the action verbs that are often used to describe the thinking habits mathematicians routinely employ: *looking* for patterns, *conjecturing*, *justifying*, *analyzing*, *wondering*, and so on. Everyone can learn these ways of thinking if given the opportunity.

Second, I believe that *teaching mathematics* means helping all students learn to think mathematically. This means setting up situations that give every student the opportunity to engage in sense making. It requires a lot of listening and questioning. It also means explicitly helping students develop attitudes about the nature of mathematics and what is required in its learning. The following paragraphs contain messages that I believe students need to hear and see in action every day.

11

- Mathematics includes arithmetic, but it is more than just arithmetic. Many middle school students have spent years practicing arithmetic algorithms and evaluating algebraic expressions but very little time engaging in the study of geometry, or probability, or data analysis, or functions. Middle school students also need to be constantly reminded that mathematical thinking is mathematics, too.

- There is no direct route to understanding. Mistakes and confusion are an essential part of this process. One of the principles that consistently guides me is this: "We must recognize that partially grasped ideas and periods of confusion are a natural part of the process of developing understanding" (California State Department of Education 1987, 14).

- There are many ways to be good at math. Being fast and accurate with procedures is one way, but other ways include being good wonderers, good visualizers, good explainers, flexible problem solvers, adept pattern finders, or facile technology users. Everyone can be good at mathematics and we need people who are good at all of those different ways in our mathematical community.

- There are many ways to approach most mathematical problems, even those with only one answer. And while some ways may appear to be more efficient than others, what is most important is that everyone has at least one way to solve a problem that she or he really understands. Mathematics should make sense.

- We can get better at the skills of mathematics through practice, but talking and listening to each other (not just the teacher) about mathematical ideas help us understand mathematical ideas in different ways. We really understand what we can explain.

In these video cases you are offered the opportunity to watch moments of lessons in which the teaching decisions and discourse that ensued were unique to this particular moment in time. We hope you will think about these lessons in the context of your own classroom, your students, and your learning. We hope they will prompt useful questions, ideas, and discussions among professionals on a common journey.

Chapter 2

Building on Student Ideas
The Border Problem, Part 1 (March 9)

From whence does algebra grow?
It grows from the study of growth itself.

DOSSEY (1997, 20)

The fact that many children cannot understand much of the algebra
we teach leads them to dislike and ultimately reject it, and thence
possibly the whole subject of mathematics.

ORTON AND FROBISHER (1996, 14)

Background of the Lesson—Cathy's Perspective

It has long been an interest of mine to find ways to make algebra more accessible. So, when I needed to select a writing project for my master's degree, it was natural that I chose algebraic representation as a topic.

The research for my project corroborated my teaching experiences. I learned that far too many students are not successful in algebra, despite its role as a gatekeeper for further mathematics study and college entrance (Silver 1997). I learned that the ideas of equality and variable are particularly thorny obstacles and that our students are often not able to apply the routine skills they have learned to problem-solving situations (Brown et al. 1988). None of these findings came as a surprise. But I also discovered that, while there is no consensus on a single best way to remedy these problems, there is general agreement that an emphasis on pattern generalization supports the development of algebraic thinking (Driscoll 1999; Haimes 1996; Lee 1996; Mason 1996; NCTM 2000; Schoenfeld and Arcavi 1988) and that the concept of function is fundamental to the ideas of algebra (Brenner et al. 1997; Leitzel 1989; Lodholz 1990; Thorpe 1989). Since pattern generalization and a functions approach that focuses on the relationship between quantities (Chazan 2000) are closely related, I decided this was the way I wanted to introduce the ideas of algebra to my seventh graders.

My experiences with using a functions-based approach in my work in professional development raised related issues for me. As my colleagues and I designed lessons based on the visualization of growth patterns for teachers in our summer workshops, I began adapting those lessons for my middle school students. To my dismay, my students, like many of the teachers in our workshops, did not have the powerful experiences I had expected. While they enjoyed the tasks and successfully completed tables of values, they faltered when they tried to write algebraic expressions to represent the relationships. The language of algebra seemed foreign and artificial; the teachers, in particular, seemed to be trying to remember what to do rather than allowing the algebraic representation to emerge from what they understood about the relationships they were investigating. This experience prompted my personal quest to learn more about how to help bring understanding to the complex world of generalization. I kept tinkering with the tasks and trying different approaches. I went to conferences, read articles and books, and talked with colleagues who were struggling with the same issues.

I came to believe that finding the algebraic rule really isn't the point. While there are many techniques to help students find an algebraic rule, Thornton (2001) argues that it is less important that students be able to find the algebraic rule than that they recognize that the different visualizations of a pattern can be described symbolically in equivalent algebraic expressions. The underlying complexity of the mathematics embedded in the problem situation can become lost—for both the teacher and the student—when finding the rule becomes the point of the exercise. As Duckworth (1991) notes in relation to poetry, people tend to notice very different things, and each of those things contributes to greater understanding for each person. "A teacher who presents a subject matter in all of its complexity makes it more accessible by opening a multiplicity of paths into it" (8–9).

Fortified by these convictions, I designed a sequence of linked lessons in which students would investigate growth patterns in order to build their understanding of algebraic representation. The lessons consisted of interesting and predictable growth patterns—all discrete polynomial functions—which the students would investigate using cubes, tiles, toothpicks, pattern blocks, and Cuisenaire Rods®. These lessons addressed the following National Council of Teachers of mathematics (NCTM) content standards, which are particularly relevant for the middle grades:

- Develop an initial conceptual understanding of different uses of variables
- Develop an initial conceptual understanding of the notion of function

- Recognize and generate equivalent forms for algebraic expressions
- Represent, analyze, and generalize a variety of linear and nonlinear functions with tables, graphs, verbal rules, and symbolic rules
- Relate and compare different representations of a function

If lists of content standards were sufficient, however, children's difficulties with algebra would have been solved long ago. I thought long and hard not only about what problems the students would work on, but about how to make my instruction yield the most benefit for students' algebraic thinking. How any activity is enacted in a classroom—and what the students learn from it—depends not only on the task itself but on the teacher's image of the essential mathematics in the task (Thomson et al. 1994). So, as I planned to teach these lessons, I thought carefully about how I would pose the problems and what teaching strategies would be the most effective in maintaining a healthy balance between allowing students to pursue their own ways of thinking and providing information to support the development of symbolic mathematics (Hiebert et al. 1997).

The Border Problem is the first lesson in my unit. Versions of this classic problem appear in many curriculum materials in which algebra is being introduced (Burns and Humphreys 1990; Fendel et al. 1997; Lappan et al. 1998b). In this problem, students are presented with some version of the diagram in Figure 2–1, in this case a 10-by-10 grid, with its "border" colored.

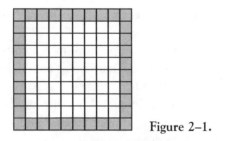

Figure 2–1.

Students are asked to calculate the number of colored squares in the border. Since there are six different ways (other than counting) to visualize how to find the number of squares in the border, the Border Problem has great potential for examining equivalent expressions. Also, since the relationship between the number of unit squares on one side of the grid and the number of unit squares in the border is a function, this problem also contains promise for establishing other important notions from which major algebraic ideas can be developed. These include the following:

- The arithmetic that emerges from the geometry of the border can be applied when the grid changes size.

- These generalized calculations can be described verbally, pictured geometrically, expressed symbolically, and represented graphically.
- The symbolic expressions that represent the particular visualizations from which they have emerged are algebraically equivalent.

I had had countless discussions with colleagues about the best way to draw out the potential in this problem. I knew what I was *not* trying to develop: I did not want to focus on simplifying expressions (yet), nor did I want students to determine the "most efficient" way of finding the number of squares in the border (efficiency is often in the eye of the beholder when it comes to mathematical thinking). That there were thirty-six squares in the border was certainly not the point, as the squares could be counted easily by any second grader. I knew that I did not want to do the students' thinking for them by showing different methods to calculate the number of squares in the border. Deborah Ball says, "With my ears to the ground, listening to my students, my eyes are focused on the mathematical horizon" (1993, 376). I set out to draw upon students' natural abilities to visualize and, in doing so, to breathe life into symbolic representation.

The Border Problem typically takes three forty-five-minute class periods. On the first day, the students generate a variety of ways to figure out the number of unit squares in the border. Their geometric visualizations serve as the "currency" (Hiebert et al. 1997) with which they will eventually build connections between the arithmetic and geometry of the function. They also are asked to imagine the grid changing size (either stretching or shrinking) with an eye toward generalization.

The purpose of the second class session is to introduce the tools of multiple representations. Using one visual method as a model, the students learn to represent that method geometrically, arithmetically, verbally, and algebraically. This is examined in more detail in Chapter 3. Finally, on the third day of their work on this problem, students choose another method and work in pairs to represent that method using the four representations they have learned.

This case begins as I introduce the problem; the segment continues as students generate and geometrically justify different calculation methods.

Watch "Building on Student Ideas: The Border Problem, Part 1," CD 1

Lesson Analysis and Reflection

As I put the slide of the grid on the overhead projector, I told the students that it was 10 by 10 and asked them to "figure out *without talking, without writing,* and *without counting one by one*" how many unit squares were in the colored portion.

Why without talking? I wanted to have as wide a variety of methods as possible, and sharing methods early on might limit the variety.

Why without writing? The numbers are well within the grasp of seventh graders, and freedom from pencils helps students enlist the power of visualization as a support to calculation.

Why without counting one by one? Although this can yield a correct answer, it is not a method that lends itself to the goals of pattern generalization. (As it turned out, one student did go to the overhead and count around one by one but ended up with the wrong answer!)

Why didn't I give them each a grid to facilitate their thinking? I have found that if students have a grid, they tend to count one by one. If counting one by one is their initial method, then sharing other ways to find the number of squares is an intellectual or creative enterprise without meaning.

My next decision was to have the students talk to each other *just* about what they got. In saying this, I meant that I first wanted them to talk about the answers they got, not yet about how they got them. I knew from experience that thirty-eight and forty are predictable answers because of compensation errors, and while I did not want the answer to divert us from the main point of the lesson, I did want to shine a light on the logic of these common errors. I use this teaching strategy to help students see mathematics as a sense-making activity and to show that we can use errors as sites for learning (Hiebert et al. 1997).

After this, students volunteered to share how they got thirty-six. I recorded their methods.

Why did I record, rather than let students do so? I wanted to model correct numerical representation for instructional advantage. I recorded all of the arithmetic expressions *horizontally* so that they could more easily be connected to the algebraic expression. I also avoided use of the equals sign; I did this to counteract the widespread interpretation of the equals sign as a "get the answer" operator and to emphasize the idea that the numerical expression represents an answer in the same way that a symbolic expression does. A student who thinks the equals sign means "write the answer" is likely to think that, for an expression like $x + y$, a single-term answer is required (e.g., $x + y = z$) (Booth 1988). I also intended to name a method after its originator; this would help distinguish one method from another in the lesson that would follow—and besides, it is nice to give credit to students for their ways of thinking.

Sharmeen was first to share; she saw the border as $4 \times 10 - 4$ (four sides of ten unit squares each minus four overlapping squares at the corners). I wish I had asked her to go to the overhead projector and show how her arithmetic made sense geometrically. Not doing so was one of those odd oversights that occur, no matter how much I think about and plan a lesson. Pressing Sharmeen to distinguish between the two 4s in her arithmetic expression, however, was a way of helping everyone in the class think about how the two 4s played a different role in the numerical expression, and it helped emphasize the connection between the numerical expression and its geometric foundation.

Colin's method was to add $10 + 9 + 9 + 8$, visualizing first one full side, then a side without one corner, and another, and the last side without two corners. In his explanation to the class, Colin not only described what he had done but justified geometrically each of the numbers in his expression. The intentional connection between arithmetic and geometry moved toward building a common understanding that whenever we make a statement about a pattern, we justify it geometrically. This idea would be foundational for all of the problems in this unit.

Joe volunteered the method that had been employed by most of the students in the class: $10 + 10 + 8 + 8$. He had counted the full top and bottom of the border, and then had subtracted two from each of the sides to account for the overlaps at the four corners. When Joe was explaining his method, I heard him say that he had added "those two" (meaning $8 + 8$) and then added that result to twenty. If I had recorded it *exactly* as he had said it, I would have recorded:

$$10 + 10 = 20$$
$$8 + 8 = 16$$
$$20 + 16 = 36$$

I did not do so because of past experience. Too many students, using the logic that a different number should represent a different letter, had attempted to generalize this same method like this:

$$a + a = x$$
$$b + b = y$$
$$x + y = z$$

I therefore deliberately wrote Joe's method as a single expression ($10 + 10 + 8 + 8$) rather than three equations. I made sure to check with him, however, to confirm that this was a fair representation of his method.

Melissa used a subtraction method to find the number of squares in the border. She saw two squares: one, a 10-by-10 grid, and the other, an 8-by-8 grid. The border was the difference of the two. I recorded Melissa's method carefully, writing $(10 \times 10) - (8 \times 8)$. Even though the parentheses were not required, I included them to emphasize the subtraction of two numbers, one-hundred and sixty-four.

Tina, who had seen the border as four overlapping lengths of nine, reported 4×9 as her method.

At this point in the lesson, one student suggested "six times six" as a method. This is a common dilemma with students who are new to classes that build on student thinking. I had taken over this class for another teacher in January and, this being early March, some students had not yet internalized the notion that mathematical sense making was essential. This student assumed that our aim here was to gather as many methods as possible, regardless of whether the methods made sense. I had a brief discussion about how, while 6×6 did indeed equal the number of squares in the border, we would not record it as a method since it did not emerge from the geometry of the border.

After the students had generated all of the methods they could think of, there was still one additional method ($4 \times 8 + 4$) that they would need for the next day's lesson. In the past I had dealt with this by asking students to think about "how else someone might see it," but this time I decided to tell them the method (saying that a student in another class, named Zach, had come up with it) and see if they could figure out why it made sense geometrically. This is an example of what Mark Driscoll, in his book *Fostering Algebraic Thinking,* calls "doing-undoing," a strategy he believes is "critical to developing power in algebraic thinking" (1999, 1). This approach proved to be interesting and engaging for this class and I was delighted that Kayla, who often lacked confidence, was eager to explain Zach's method.

With all of the methods now on the board, I had planned to have students think about changing the size of the grid. But Kay's striking observation that Tina's and Zach's methods were alike changed the course of my lesson, taking it to a deeper level of analysis. My original plan had been to have the students mentally stretch and shrink the grid, but making connections among methods and how they are alike and different begins to lay the foundation for the concept of algebraic equivalence. In other words, the numerical expressions are equivalent not only because they generate the same number of squares but because their *structures* have similarities and differences that compensate for each other. Kay's comment was one of those gifts to classroom interaction that turn up more frequently as students gain faith in their own reasoning, and it triggered similar observations about the other methods.

After thinking about connections among all of the methods on the board, there was still time for the students to think about changing the size of the square. I was momentarily uncertain whether the students should all use a particular method or each use their own method; while each person's own method might be more accessible, a single approach would be easier to discuss as a class. I decided on accessibility, asking students to use their own method to visualize a 6-by-6 grid. I anticipated that there would be clusters of students who had used each method. Sharmeen's method, $4 \times 10 - 4$, was the first on our list of methods, so I asked the class, "What would Sharmeen have done?" as a way to help students apply her method to any size grid—a stepping-stone to our work of generalization.

After the video selection, Shelley, the first one to answer this question, initially made a mistake in the numbers she used, saying "Six times ten minus six" and then "four times six minus six." It was evident that Shelley was looking at number patterns rather than the geometry of the method:

10 by 10:	Sharmeen:	$4 \times 10 - 4$
6 by 6:	Shelley, first try:	$6 \times 10 - 6$
	Shelley, second try:	$4 \times 6 - 6$
	Shelley, final explanation:	$4 \times 6 - 4$

I did not correct Shelley because I was more interested in letting her figure out her own error. Many of the students were eager to correct her, but when she started to explain the reasoning behind $6 \times 10 - 6$, she changed her idea to $4 \times 6 - 6$. This prompted her classmates to raise their hands again. But when Shelley began to justify $4 \times 6 - 6$, she again changed her answer, this time to $4 \times 6 - 4$ (for the corners). This demonstrates how student errors illuminate student thinking and how important it is for people to have the opportunity to correct their own mistakes. The period was nearly over, but I planned to revisit this problem in more depth the next day.

Case Commentary—Jo's Analysis

The Implementation of Tasks

"What I would like you to do mentally is figure out, without counting one by one, how many squares are in the colored portion. How many unit squares—and without talking, without counting one by one, without writing it."

These are the words with which Cathy started the lesson. An uninformed observer might think that such precise instructions are not needed—why didn't Cathy just ask the students to work out how many squares were in the border?

Why did she show the border on the overhead and not give the students their own copies to work from? But Cathy's words and actions were carefully planned and they were important for encouraging the many methods and connections that emerged. Another teacher once watched the case and saw the wonderful work the students were doing and the excitement they had in seeing different methods. She decided to try the activity in her classroom, but she was teaching a group of students that she perceived as weak, so she gave them their own copies of the border to work with. When the teacher asked the students how many squares were on the border, they looked at their papers and counted. The teacher went on to ask the students for their methods for working out the number of squares, but nobody had any methods to share and the students couldn't see the point of the activity. This event illustrated for me the huge importance of *task implementation*—the decisions teachers make as they present tasks in the classroom. Stein, Smith, Henningsen, and Silver (2000) wrote an important book in which they presented different cases of task implementation. They showed that the same task could be implemented at a number of different levels, and that frequently teachers use open tasks with the hope that they will inspire student thinking, but close the tasks down to the point that students can answer them with minimal cognitive effort. In Stein and her colleagues' words, the cognitive demand of tasks is frequently lowered. Cathy carefully chose the words and actions with which she started the lesson to maintain a high level of thinking and to generate the wonderful range of methods the students produced in the case.

Detailed Planning

How did a task that may appear trivial on paper explode into such a broad array of methods and unexpectedly complex connections? This came about, in part, because Cathy had planned so carefully and she was purposefully using the task as a means to generate methods that could be expressed algebraically and that could lead into discussions of equivalence. The mathematical meanings that were developed in the first two cases (and more generally in the entire unit of work) demonstrate the importance of planning across time—of developing a series of linked lessons that purposefully introduce students to ideas and then build upon them. Some people may look at this case and think it is a nice example of students sharing ideas and methods, but it is more than that. It is also the start of a mathematical journey that will take students into the realms of algebraic equivalence and the representation of functions. The case may also look like an instance of students sharing any methods they happened to use, but it is not; it is a teacher purposefully drawing out six particular different methods. The fact that Cathy was able to look for those methods, and even bring in another method that had not been raised by her class and ask students to work "backwards" (Driscoll 1999) to visualize it, was testament to her careful planning of the lessons (Ball 1993).

Connecting Representations

A number of interesting events transpired in the course of the lesson. One moment I find particularly significant was when Cathy showed Zach's method and asked the students why it made sense with the diagram. As students looked at Zach's method and at the grid, we started to hear choruses of "Ooh," "Aah," and "Oh, I see it!" Those are the sounds of mathematical wonder—the students were curious about the way Zach's method worked, they were pleased when they could see it, and they experienced some of the joy of a mathematical breakthrough. These are the sorts of moments that mathematics classrooms should be full of, but they rarely happen. In the quote that opens this book, Margaret Wertheim's (1997) description of the "secret image" of pi, the "treasure of the universe that had just been revealed," reminds us both of the mystery and intrigue of mathematics and the natural wonder of children. Classrooms should be full of such moments, as we pique children's interest and surprise them with the connections and relationships that make mathematics so special. Since it is unlikely that students will experience such insights by plowing through worksheets that require them to repeat procedures, we must create such moments in more engaging and interactive ways. Seeing a mathematical expression represented in a diagram should not be a rare source of wonder for students, they should receive many opportunities to explore the relationships between geometric and algebraic forms. For some students it is a source of surprise that such connections can even be made. In this classroom the expressions of "Ooh," "Aah," and "Cool" as students considered the different representations of the border told us that they had experienced some of the mathematical insight and wonder that Wertheim so powerfully describes.

Connecting Different Methods

Another interesting moment in the lesson came when Kay commented that Zach's method was like Tina's, "only that (it was) eight times four and not nine times four." This led into a discussion in which students compared and contrasted the different methods. Kay demonstrated in that moment the classroom practice she had learned of looking for the connections among different methods. This is an extremely important mathematical practice. After the students discussed the connections among methods, Cathy asked them to shrink the square in their minds and to use one of the methods to find the number of squares in the border of the new square. This is an interesting task as it can be solved only by linking the particular mathematical expression to the imagined square, which involves high levels of visualization and reasoning. This act of connecting a prealgebraic expression to a geometric representation is extremely valuable. Mark Driscoll (1999) talks about the importance of appreciating the *form* of algebraic expressions, as algebraic expressions of different forms give insights into different aspects of mathematical relationships. For example, the expression $4 \times n - 4$ for representing the squares in the border of a grid with side length n shows something different than the expression $n + (n - 1) + (n - 1) + (n - 2)$. If the value of different expressions is partly determined by the insights they show, then their form becomes critically important. This task is cultivating an appreciation of algebraic form.

Similarly, earlier in the lesson, when students were looking to see where certain numbers were represented on the diagram, they were being encouraged to appreciate that algebra is a *tool* for representing a mathematical relationship, rather than a result. Noss, Healy, and Hoyles (1997) point out that somewhere along the way, we stopped viewing algebra as a set of problem-solving tools and now regard it as an end point. Fiori (2004) makes a similar point, noting an interesting reversal of cause and effect: problems have become a resource for practicing algebra, instead of algebra being learned and used as a tool for exploring problems.

The students in this class had an interesting day—they saw that mathematical expressions represent something real, and they marveled at the links between written expressions and visual representations. Their appreciation of the mathematics was tangible and the scene was set for their first encounter with variables.

Chapter 3

Building Understanding of Algebraic Representation
The Border Problem, Part 2 (March 12)

Visualization . . . is one of the most rapidly growing areas of mathematics and scientific research. Learning to visualize mathematical patterns enlists the gift of sight as an invaluable ally in mathematical education.

Steen (1990, 6)

Background of the Lesson—Cathy's Perspective

The Border Problem is the first problem in a sequence of lessons I designed for seventh graders. Students learn to use algebraic notation to represent growth patterns by relying on their ability to visualize what the pattern would look like at any stage of growth. As the unit progresses, students build proficiency with tables, graphs, symbolic rules, and verbal rules. While I knew that understanding the connections among these representations is crucial for attaining flexibility and competence with algebraic expressions (NCTM 2000), I had also learned from my research that the ability to move freely among these representations is essential for conceptual development of functions (Brenner et al. 1997; Hollar and Norwood 1999; Kieran 1992; Ritchhart 1997; Van Dyke and Craine 1997). And because functions are so important in higher mathematics, I also devised lessons that would develop explicit connections among the different representations to lay the groundwork for future understandings.

On the first day of the Border Problem, as seen in Chapter 2, the students generated different ways of visualizing the number of unit squares in the border of a 10-by-10 grid. They also began to think about how the six equivalent arithmetic expressions were alike and different and began to imagine stretching and shrinking the grid. I found the introductory lesson to be interesting and accessible for the students, but now the real work of connecting their thinking to the underlying mathematics of generalization and multiple representations would begin. In this lesson, I planned to introduce students to four different representations (geometric, numeric, verbal, and algebraic) for the functional relationship between the length of the side of a grid and the number of unit squares in the grid's border.

In most curriculum materials involving growth patterns, the table of values, often called an *in-out table*, is normally the first representation that students are given; they fill in the table and then look for patterns. Yet I made a deliberate decision not to introduce this particular representation in the early lessons of this unit. Why did I make this decision? For many students, patterns of the dependent variable in an ordered table—what is added for each stage of growth—obscure the relationship *between* the variables. In other words, students often focus on the *pattern* rather than the *function*. While recursive analysis is certainly useful as a window into how a function behaves, I prefer to introduce this tool later in students' experiences. Early emphasis on the table of values can also make students think that finding the rule is the goal of the lesson. To the contrary, the aim of the lessons as I have envisioned them is for students to be able to write algebraic expressions that represent particular visualizations. The point is not to find the rule—especially a simplified rule!—but rather to represent symbolically what they *see*. The different visualizations provide a springboard from which students can grapple with equivalence and they bring life to what otherwise might be strings of meaningless symbols.

In order to express their methods algebraically, students would need to learn to use variables. I was fairly certain that any prior experience my students had had with variables was limited to evaluating variable expressions and/or finding the value of unknowns in simple equations. But NCTM (2000) states, "Students' understanding of variable should go far beyond simply recognizing that letters can be used to stand for unknown numbers in equations" (225). And from my research I had learned that the concept of variable is much more complex than I had realized, and that it "frequently turns out to be *the* concept that blocks students' success in algebra" (Leitzel 1989, 29). I discovered that misconceptions about variables are resistant to change and often are exacerbated by instruction and instructional materials.

The most pervasive misconception students have about variables, for example, is that letters are *initials* or *labels* (e.g., *a* as a label for apples rather than the *number* of apples) (Booth 1988; Pegg and Redden 1990; Wagner 1983; Wagner and Kieran 1989; Wagner and Parker 1993). I was somewhat dismayed to realize this, as in the past I had used *b* to represent the number of squares in the border. But the knowledge helped me be explicit that the independent variable in this problem would represent the *number* of squares in the border, no matter what variable I used. Students also commonly think that different letters in an expression cannot represent the same number (Booth 1988) or that changing a letter changes the solution (Wagner 1983). With this last misconception in mind, I decided that I should not choose a variable for the students but that they all should select a letter of their choice.

The other helpful bit of research I found was that students' understanding of the equals sign as a "get the answer" symbol is an obstacle for seeing an expression as an answer (Wheeler 1996, 324). This misconception is understandable, since most (if not all) of students' experiences in arithmetic have taught them to interpret the equals sign as a signal to "write the answer" (Booth 1988; Kieran 1992; Kieran and Chalouh 1993; Wagner and Parker 1993) or that it means "makes" (Stacey and MacGregor 1997). So another of my challenges would be to help students understand that the expression itself was an answer.

Prior to the Video Selection

I chose to use Joe's method, $10 + 10 + 8 + 8$, as a model for the four representations the students would be introduced to that day. I began the lesson by asking students to visualize a 6-by-6 square grid and think about what Joe would do to find the number of unit squares in its border. I made it clear that I was not as interested in *how many* unit squares were in the border as I was in *what Joe would have done* to figure it out. When Sarah responded, I recorded on the overhead what she said without including the total number of squares:

$$\text{6-by-6:}\quad 6 + 6 + 4 + 4$$

Next I had the students imagine stretching the grid to 15 by 15. Could they use Joe's method for this size grid? They agreed that they could; Shelley volunteered that Joe would have added $15 + 15 + 13 + 13$. I recorded this directly under what I had written for the 6-by-6 grid. Because these examples seemed so straightforward for the students, I decided to test their flexibility by using a much larger grid. I asked if they thought they would be able to use Joe's method for a 233-by-233 grid. Several students chorused $233 + 233 + 231 + 231$, and when I asked them if they thought they could apply Joe's method to *any* size grid, they eagerly agreed that they could. This kind of experience gives students a glimpse into the power of functions and I find it very exciting to be with them when this happens.

I wrote $233 + 233 + 231 + 231$ on the overhead and told the students that this was one way to represent and analyze the relationship between the length of the side of the grid and the number of unit squares in the border; I called it the arithmetic representation.

Arithmetic:	
10-by-10:	10 + 10 + 8 + 8
6-by-6:	6 + 6 + 4 + 4
15-by-15:	15 + 15 + 13 + 13
233-by-233:	233 + 233 + 231 + 231

Figure 3–1.

Figure 3–1 shows what was written on the overhead projector at that point. I asked students to copy this into their notebooks; this would serve as a model for work they would do individually.

Next, I drew a "generic" square (see Figure 3–2) to represent Joe's method geometrically, coloring it as shown, while they copied it.

In order to make an explicit connection between the two representations they had learned so far, I went back to the arithmetic of the 15-by-15 grid (15 + 15 + 13 + 13) and asked the students where the 15 was in the generic square, and where the 13 was, and why. I continued with questioning like this in order to help establish students' flexibility with moving between the two representations. They seemed confident, and using Joe's method seemed clear, so I thought we were ready to tackle the verbal representation.

The verbal representation is the hardest for me to introduce, and it is tempting to go directly to the algebraic representation, which somehow seems easier! Once again, however, research guided my decision making. I had learned that verbal statements about functional relationships are critical for understanding (Brenner et al. 1997; Dossey 1997; NCTM 2000; Van Dyke and Craine 1997) and that it is important to make sure students verbalize generalizations of patterns before asking them to formalize those generalizations symbolically. In asking students to write a verbal rule, however, I wanted more than a direct translation; I wanted the students to remain cognizant of the geometric roots of each part of

Geometic:

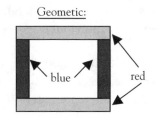

Figure 3–2.

their verbal rule. So, for example, instead of them just saying, "Subtract two," I wanted students to write something like, "Subtract two *for the overlapping unit squares on the corners*," to keep their thinking grounded in geometry. I hoped this would have the effect of building sense making in algebraic representation; I wanted them to see that each operation and each number means something particular and important in an expression.

I plunged ahead, asking students to think about how we could "write directions" that someone could easily follow to apply Joe's method. "What is the first thing Joe would do?" I asked.

Stephanie responded, "Take the number of unit squares on one side."

I was alert to the potential problems with the word *side*, as it could refer to either a position on the square (i.e., side as opposed to top or bottom) or *any* side. After clarifying that she meant on any side ("because all of the sides are the same length in a square"), I wrote this on the overhead transparency. "What next?" I inquired.

Sarah said, "Add that number to itself."

I asked where that made sense with the picture, and she responded, "For the top and bottom," which I recorded in parentheses. I asked students to think about how this sentence related to the generic grid I had drawn; Dana thought it was the "red part," and many students nodded in agreement.

"What next?" I asked. "What would Joe do next?" I asked the students to talk to each other in their small groups. After a few minutes I called on Colin, who said we should "subtract two from the other sides." I clarified the language a little, talking about how important it was to be clear when writing about mathematics, and recorded it this way: "Subtract two from each of the remaining sides. . . ." I then asked, "Why do we subtract two?"

Several students said, "For the corners." We had a lot of trouble here, getting the language just right. Some students wanted to say, "for the overlapping sides," but I pointed out that that didn't tell how much of each side was overlapping. With many students contributing (and some tuning out), we finally settled on this:

> Take the number of unit squares on one side. Add that number to itself (for the top and bottom). Subtract two from each of the remaining sides (for the overlapping ~~sides~~ unit squares on the corners). ~~Add the last two numbers.~~ Add these two numbers to the previous ~~number~~ sum.

The students then copied this into their notebooks under the heading, "Verbal." As the clip begins, I move to the algebraic representation by having the students consider how to "shorten" the verbal representation.

Watch "Building Understanding of Algebraic Representation: The Border Problem, Part 2," CD 1

Lesson Analysis and Reflection

When I asked how mathematicians might "shorten" the verbal description and still communicate Joe's method, Krysta seemed excited about the idea of using algebra. Her statement that mathematicians would "make the fifteens xs and the thirteens ys" to "put it all in letters" alerted me to a mistaken assumption that I had seen among my students in the past: that an algebraic expression replaces *all* of the numbers with letters. For example, in translating Sharmeen's method for the number of squares in the border ($4 \times 10 - 4$), a student might write $x \times y - x$ and then say that $x = 4$. These students, in mechanically replacing numbers with letters, show that they do not understand—yet—the language of algebra.

I immediately used Krysta's idea to introduce the term *variable*. Not all literal symbols take the role of variables, but literal symbols are so commonly called variables (whether their role is of a variable or not) that I felt compelled to say, as I was writing *variable* on the board, that the word "does not say everything about what they do." As I wrote the word, I heard Pam say, "I knew that!" I could tell the students liked the idea of doing algebra, which has special status as a rite of passage in middle school.

I then became uncertain about how to proceed. I had already decided that students should individually choose a variable in order to counteract the potential misconception, discussed earlier, that changing the letter changes the value of the expression. If everyone used the same variable, however, the class model for the algebraic representation would be more straightforward. I was momentarily unsure but decided on the former, figuring that the students would be able to easily adapt their own variable to what was written on the overhead. And, as expected, I got into a little trouble when I tried to do the class model; at first I was going to leave a space for the variable but then realized the obvious fact that I could not write an expression without one. So I chose x, while reminding the students that they should choose their own. The uncertainty that is evident in this vignette occurs every so often in my practice. The more I learn—about mathematics, about my students, about teaching itself—the more choices I have in the moment-to-moment decisions that a teacher must make in every lesson. The notion that there is one right, best way, what Chazan (2000) calls "a vocabulary of certainty," to approach a topic every time is foreign to me. Chazan continues, "Just as an overreliance on the categories of 'right' and 'wrong' inhibits discussion in mathematics classrooms, a technical vocabulary of certainty inhibits discussion of teaching practice" (153). I often will purposely make different decisions in the same lesson with different classes. For me, it is so important to study and discuss with my colleagues the effects of different teaching moves; it is one of the things that makes teaching fascinating.

I also needed to decide whether to define the variable for the students or let them figure it out. I might have asked, "What does Joe need to know in order to find the number of unit squares in the border?" or "What should the variable represent?" and, indeed, I have followed that path with other classes. In *this* class and at *this* time, however, I decided to postpone the issue of how to define an independent variable in order to allow as much of the twelve or so remaining minutes for students to work together to use algebra as a "convenient shorthand for expressing ideas with which they have already grappled" (Schoenfeld and Arcavi 1988, 425–26).

Why didn't I just *show* students the correct way to write the algebraic expression? I could have written $x + x + (x - 2) + (x - 2)$, explaining clearly why the subtraction made sense. On its face, this approach seems more efficient; I could have believed that I had taught it and the students could have believed that they had learned it. But one of my major goals for these lessons was to have students learn to represent relationships algebraically—for themselves. I doubted that writing the expression for them would generate the tools and understandings they would need to solve problems that they had not yet seen. I have come to believe that relationships cannot be taught, but rather that "relationships are constructed, or made, by each individual" (Kamii and Warrington 1999, 83). Writing the algebraic expression for Joe's method requires students to consider how to represent two numbers that are related by a difference of two. Learning to represent that relationship is crucial for building sense making in algebraic representation.

I set the stage for them to write the algebraic expression by telling students that the first sentence (in their verbal representation) was important because it told "what Joe need[ed] to know to figure out the number of unit squares [in the border]." I proceeded to write, letting x be "the number of unit squares on one side," and I directed students to work together to "translate [the verbal representation] into an algebra expression," pointing out the verbal, geometric, and arithmetic representations that were visible as models on the overhead. What happened next was a direct result of my recent reading of Mark Driscoll's book *Fostering Algebraic Thinking* (1999). In his book, Driscoll recommends that teachers focus students' attention on what is staying the same and what is changing in order to help them learn how to build rules to represent functions. I directed the students' attention toward our arithmetic examples and asked them, "What's staying the same in this arithmetic?"

Pam volunteered, "You're always adding."

There was very little interest in this question, so I asked what was changing. Sarah noticed that "the first two numbers are the same and the last two numbers are the same." She did not mention that there was always a difference of two between the first two addends and the last two addends, but again I made a decision not to press the students about this but rather to let them ponder it on their own. The impact of these questions surfaced later in the lesson.

As the students worked in their groups to write algebraic expressions, I visited a few groups to get a sense of how students were doing. My goal was not to correct students' errors or to put them on the right track but rather to ask questions and find out how they were thinking. This process helps me ferret out issues that would be good for class discussions or further work and it keeps students responsible for their thinking. As I walked around the classroom, I was drawn to the discussion Joe, Kayla, Pam, and Mindy were having; they were wondering whether they should use a different letter to represent the length of the remaining sides. An important convention in algebraic representation is that if there is a predictable relationship between numbers, we generally write one in terms of the other. This is a new idea for middle school students and a big leap for many because they rarely have the opportunity to encounter this idea in their textbooks.

The luxury of a videotaped lesson is that the camera offers a kind of eye in the back of the classroom. While the students were working in small groups, Antony, Sharmeen, and Kim had an interesting interaction that I learned about only while watching the tape. Sharmeen had a correct expression ($s + s + s - 2 + s - 2$) but erased it immediately when Kim said, "No. . . . " Watching the tape, I was dismayed at how quickly Sharmeen erased her work, that she did not ask why Kim thought her expression was wrong, and that Kim did not ask Sharmeen why she thought her expression made sense. It made me realize how easy it is to succumb to the assumption that group work is productive if there is a reasonably businesslike sound in the room. This incident underscored for me the importance of explicitly establishing and reinforcing class norms for group work; in this case, my students needed to establish the expectation that they would always give reasons for their answers.

This small interaction also demonstrated how students view what is simple versus what is complicated in algebraic expressions. Sharmeen read her expression ($s + s + s - 2 + s - 2$) to her group apologetically, saying she thought it was "complicated," not realizing that it was correct. Kim later said she also thought Sharmeen's expression was "really complicated." If I view this through their eyes, $s + s + k + k$ *looks* a lot simpler, maybe because there are less characters or because the 2s aren't there. I had, after all, asked students to "shorten" their verbal statements. Writing one number, $s - 2$, in terms of another, s, is indeed a different way of thinking about what is simpler.

In class, I overheard the end of this conversation and decided to stop the class. Hoping to promote a discussion that would raise this issue for everyone to consider, I began by asking Pam if she would be willing to tell the class her theory (that they needed a second variable). After Pam spoke, though, I realized that not everyone understood what Pam had meant. I called on Travis, who thought he understood it but couldn't get the words out. So I went back to Pam to restate her idea then her groupmate Joe called on Stephanie to respond.

When Stephanie explained that it could be done with one variable, the timer rang, indicating five minutes to go in class; there was also the suggestion of widespread agreement with what she had said. I asked, "Why does that work? Why does that make sense?" Melissa's explanation focused on what was important—that all of the sides of the square grid were the same length, so we didn't need another letter. I wanted everyone to think about this: "When do you need another letter, and when don't you?" I knew that some of the tasks students would be tackling would require two independent variables, and I wanted to raise the issue and emphasize its importance. I was really surprised, then, when Pam commented that my earlier question about what was staying the same and what was changing had confused her. And she noticed something important: that "in the algebraic formula the things that are the same and different are not the same things that are the same and different on the numbers."

I was thankful not only that Pam had been able to put those thoughts into words but that she had so willingly expressed them. So often I am reminded of a perceptive statement by Daniel Chazan: "Student centered teaching makes the teacher all the more dependent on students. Not only were we dependent on our students to learn, but we also depended on them to help produce classroom interaction, or our lessons could come to a grinding halt" (2000, 120). It had not occurred to me that my question would lead some students into thinking that if you needed a different number, then you would need a different letter. But I was glad the light had shone so brightly that day on an issue that would come up again and again.

Sarah's algebraic expression at the end of the clip raised the issue of equivalence, which I took up with the students in another lesson. This lesson ended with Travis stating a correct algebraic expression to represent the relationship between the number of unit squares on one side and the number of unit squares in the border.

The Next Day

The next day, students worked in pairs to investigate and represent a second method arithmetically, geometrically, verbally, and algebraically. At the end of class, I collected their papers and read them carefully so that I could use their work as examples to help all of the students build their capacity for expressing relationships algebraically.

Postscript

About a month later I received an email from Kay, one of the students in this class. She was working on one of the last problems in our unit, which had different levels of difficulty. The level she was working on required three independent variables, one for length, one for width, and one for height. She wrote, "I have a question about the toothpick problem . . . If we were doing the expert level, we can only use 2 variables for each equation, right? Thanks."

This showed me how difficult the concept of variable really is for students. The idea that the length, width, and height of any rectangular prism are not related was not the issue for her; it was an issue of how many variables they were *supposed* to use. I was surprised by this question, but it helped me understand the complexity of the idea of dependence. Later, in her portfolio entry on this task, Kay wrote, "What this shows about me mathematically: This shows that I still wanted to use an extra variable, but I tried really hard not to."

Case Commentary—Jo's Analysis

Forming Algebraic Expressions

On the second day of the Border Problem, students made their way into the complex world of algebraic representation. We saw some initial conceptions and thoughts, most of them naïve and many of them expressed with uncertainty as students worked at the edge of their understanding. We saw a teacher making every effort to guide her students through some intricate terrain, making sure that she honored their thinking while also helping them avoid some pitfalls and misconceptions (Bouvier 1987; Nesher 1987). As often happened in this class, a discussion ensued in which students were clearly both curious and involved. The discussion addressed an important and often neglected area—that of *forming* algebraic expressions (Kieran 1992). Instead of starting algebra in the more conventional way—by telling students that, h, for example, represented hours and asking students to evaluate expressions when h was a number (Brown et al. 2000)—Cathy asked the students how they could shorten a written expression to communicate the same ideas "without all the writing." The students offered tentative ideas, giving us the opportunity to hear their first conceptions of algebra. A foundation was laid for the representational system that is at the heart of mathematics and that would aid students in their future inquiries into mathematical connections and relationships.

The Importance of Misconceptions

In the discussion that took place, students communicated a number of naïve conceptions. They said, for example, that it was OK to replace numbers with letters, but they didn't know what to do with an expression such as "subtract two." The students told us that $s + s + k + k$ was simpler than $s + s + (s - 2) + (s - 2)$. These ideas are reasonable; indeed, they make perfect sense given the experiences these students had had to date. In some respects, $s + s + k + k$ is simpler and the students had learned that simplicity was good. They had yet to learn another mathematical appreciation—that capturing the relationships between numbers while avoiding the use of additional variables is mathematically important. Some people worry about students hearing misconceptions, thinking that students will remember the wrong idea rather than the correct one. But research tells us that students learn a lot when they consider competing ideas, even when some of them are wrong (Bransford, Brown, and Cocking 2000). When learners consider competing ideas, they engage in cognitive conflict and such conflict promotes learning more than the passive reception of ideas that are always correct and seem straightforward (Fredricks, Blumenfeld, and Paris 2004). We also know that it is important for teachers to consider what students know, paying "attention to the incomplete understandings, the false beliefs, and the naïve renditions of concepts that learners bring with them to a given subject" (Bransford, Brown, and Cocking 1999, 10). When Cathy encouraged students to share their initial ideas, she both gained access to the students' understandings, which she could then address through teaching, and she encouraged students to consider the validity and appropriateness of different algebraic expressions.

The discussion that took place in this lesson came from a relatively open question that Cathy asked: "How can we shorten Joe's written method?" The openness of the question gave students room to struggle with important ideas, such as ways to express a relationship and the need for new variables. Although the students struggled, they did not become anxious or disheartened. This was partly because Cathy had worked to establish classroom norms that valued exploration and even "wrong answers" (see student interviews on CD 2 for their reflections on this). The students were also confident and involved because their struggle was a collective one. We had the opportunity to watch the students work together as they navigated new terrain, learning new ideas, and their journey was, as always, an interesting one.

Focusing upon Functional Dependency

Cathy had a particular goal when planning her lesson: She wanted to encourage students to notice a relationship between the different numbers in each expression. In the early stages of the lesson the class was looking at three sets of numbers: $10 + 10 + 8 + 8$, $15 + 15 + 13 + 13$, and $6 + 6 + 4 + 4$. Cathy asked the following question (which she later regretted): "What's staying the same in this arithmetic?" She was looking for an appreciation of *functional dependency* (Kieran 1992)—an awareness that there was a relationship between the two different numbers in each expression. It is not surprising that Cathy was hoping for such awareness; she wrote in her background notes that she did not want students to

x	y
1	1
2	4
3	9
4	16

Figure 3–3.

begin this lesson by listing numbers in a table looking down the columns for recursive insights. For example, with the function $y = x^2$ students often form lists and consider each vertical column of numbers separately, saying that the first column (x) goes down in ones and the second (y) adds two more each time ($+ 3, + 5, + 7$). (See Figure 3–3.) Cathy wanted students to see more and to start to become accustomed to finding relations between members of the domain and their image. But the students did not communicate such an awareness; when Cathy asked what was the same in the expression, they offered answers such as "You are always adding." This was true, but it did not convey what Cathy was looking for. What should a teacher do in such a situation? One possibility would have been for Cathy to ask the same question again or to ask the question in a different way. When Sarah said, "Well, the first two numbers are the same numbers and the last two numbers are the same," Cathy could have asked Sarah about the relationship between them. But she chose to curtail her line of questioning and to move along, asking students to write an algebraic expression. Later Cathy tried to probe students about the relationship again, when Stephanie said that "you could just keep the same letter," Cathy asked, "Why does that work?" By the end of the lesson students were starting to form an awareness of the relationship articulated by Melissa, who told us that "all the sides are the same lengths, so that when you use one letter, you have to subtract two." But the lesson was drawing to a close at this point and the ideas were left to be developed on another day.

Was the question "What is staying the same?" the wrong one to ask at that time? Although Cathy did not get an answer she was looking for, I think it was a good question, partly because she asked the students to think in important ways about mathematical relations and they will have been encouraged to do such thinking, and also because Cathy was modeling for students the practice of asking mathematically worthwhile questions (Driscoll 1999) of their work (see Chapter 6).

The Role of Teacher Questions

In this extract we saw a teacher working to develop a critical concept through questioning. The concept was that of functional dependency—the relations between members of the domain and their image. Many research studies (e.g.,

Hiebert and Wearne 1993) have shown that teachers often fall into a trap of asking low-level questions that are not especially demanding and do not target key concepts. In a research study at Stanford, our team[1] investigated different high school mathematics approaches, monitoring students through four years of high school as they experienced different approaches (Boaler 2003a). One of the findings from that study was the critical role played by teachers' questions in the establishment of particular instructional environments as well as the mathematical *directions* of lessons (Boaler and Brodie 2004). As students work on mathematics problems in lessons, they traverse different sections of the mathematical terrain (Greeno 1991). Sometimes their paths are rather narrow—they may be led down a series of steps, without ever stopping to look at the broader landscape around them. Sometimes students wander unproductively around, never getting a sense of where they are in the terrain. The questions teachers ask guide students through particular pathways in the mathematical environment. In our analyses of lessons that start from the same task, we find that some teachers ask surface questions that do not take students deeper into mathematical issues; we think of those students as walking on a path that surrounds a beautiful forest without ever stepping into the forest to look at the trees. Other teachers ask questions that are more probing but that do not build carefully toward key concepts. We think of these students as stepping in and out of the forest, catching glimpses of trees and flowers but not learning where they are in relation to each other or how they may navigate their way through the forest. Other teachers ask questions that target key concepts and build carefully to enable students to find their way around. Those students experience the forest fully—they walk through, looking at the trees and flowers, and they also climb some trees and look at the whole terrain, getting a sense of where they are. The initial tasks that teachers use are critical in setting up the particular terrain that students will explore, but the questions that teachers use to guide students become the pathways that students walk along and that shape their experience of the terrain.

In our observations of hundreds of hours of lessons, we have noticed that teachers ask a range of question types. Previous analyses of question types have tended to divide questions rather simplistically into open and closed questions, or higher- and lower-order questions (for exceptions, see Hiebert and Wearne 1993; Driscoll 1999). But such categorizations do not seem to capture the nuance of the teaching act. Our categories are derived from an analysis of practice—we did not invent the categories *a priori*; we studied different examples of teaching and attempted to describe and name the different types of questions we recorded (see Table 1). Some of our category names draw on work by Driscoll (1999).

---

[1]Jo Boaler, Karin Brodie, Jennifer Dibrienza, Nick Fiori, Melissa Gresalfi, Emily Shahan, Megan Staples, and Toby White

Table 1: Teacher Questions

Question Type	Description	Examples
1. Gathering information, checking for a method, leading students through a method	Wants direct answer, usually wrong or right Rehearses known facts or procedures Enables students to state facts or procedures	What is the value of *x* in this equation? How would you plot that point?
2. Inserting terminology	Once ideas are under discussion, enables correct mathematical language to be used to talk about them	What is this called in mathematics? How would we write this correctly mathematically?
3. Exploring mathematical meanings and relationships	Points to underlying mathematical relationships and meanings. Makes links between mathematical ideas	Where is this *x* on the diagram? What does *probability* mean?
4. Probing; getting students to explain their thinking	Clarifies student thinking Enables students to elaborate their thinking for their own benefit and for the class	How did you get ten? Can you explain your idea?
5. Generating discussion	Enables other members of class to contribute and comment on ideas under discussion	Is there another opinion about this? What did you say, Justin?
6. Linking and applying	Points to relationships among mathematical ideas and mathematics and other areas of study or life	In what other situations could you apply this? Where else have we used this?
7. Extending thinking	Extends the situation under discussion, where similar ideas may be used	Would this work with other numbers?
8. Orienting and focusing	Helps students focus on key elements or aspects of the situation in order to enable problem solving	What is the problem asking you? What is important about this?
9. Establishing context	Talks about issues outside of math in order to enable links to be made with mathematics at later point	What is the lottery? How old do you have to be to play the lottery?

Some of these questions are worth explaining further. Type 1 questions (gathering information) are extremely common in mathematics classrooms. In our analyses of teachers using different approaches, these questions occurred frequently in classrooms using traditional and reform approaches, but they were particularly common in the more traditional classrooms. Indeed, analyses of more than twenty hours of lessons revealed that 95 percent of questions in the traditional classrooms were type 1. Teachers using reform approaches asked many more probing (type 4) questions; when students told them something, these teachers often asked how they knew or asked them to explain further. These are important questions, requiring that students justify and reason. But the question type that is arguably the most important of all—type 3, targeting key concepts—was observed very rarely. We called this question type "exploring mathematical meanings and relationships." Such questions orient students to the central mathematical ideas. They do not necessarily follow up on students' ideas; they often come from the teacher, and they serve a very particular and deliberate purpose: challenging students to consider a critical mathematical concept. Despite its importance, this type of question could not be used exclusively, and the range we have witnessed is very useful in helping students develop understandings, manipulate methods, learn vocabulary, and so on. But the questions that target mathematical meanings and relationships are critical, and surprisingly rare.

While the aim of this lesson was to express relationships algebraically and to begin to use algebraic variables, a central concept was that of functional dependency. A number of Cathy's questions were those we would code as type 3, as they targeted this concept; for example:

> What's staying the same in this arithmetic?
> Do you think you need to create another letter?
> When do you need another letter and when don't you?
> Why don't you need another letter in this case?

These questions are not about vocabulary, they are not asking for the execution of a procedure, and they are not assessing something *related to* the functional dependency, such as some arithmetic involved; rather, they directly target the concept. It is also noteworthy that Cathy had planned to ask students these questions as she prepared the lesson. Cathy knew that when she asked students to find shorter ways to write Joe's method, they would begin to use algebra and that they would stumble across the important issue of when to use more than one variable. While she may not have planned the exact wording of her questions, Cathy's careful planning, her depth of content knowledge, and her knowledge of student conceptions, ideas, and understandings combined to form these questions. Knowing to ask a question such as "when do you need another letter and when don't you?"

is an example of pedagogical content knowledge, which derives from a number of sources, including—in Cathy's case—the reading of texts on student understandings, reflection on student thinking, and the act of careful lesson planning. These questions played an important role in the lesson—they took students into critical mathematical territory and enabled them to consider the relationships there. They may not have been the best options and readers may want to consider what would have been a more ideal trajectory for the lesson, but these types of questions play a significant role in shaping the environment of the class and taking students into important mathematical terrain. I have highlighted the questions asked in this particular lesson, but teacher questions are important to all of the cases in this book and readers may wish to focus upon the questions asked in different cases.

Chapter 4

Defending Reasonableness
Division of Fractions (February 6)

My main goal was to make it possible for everyone in the class, no matter what their capacity for performing calculations or remembering terms and procedures, to study mathematical reasoning and to use mathematical reasoning to study content.

LAMPERT (2001, 65)

Background of the Lesson—Cathy's Perspective

Helping students understand division of fractions can be treacherous territory for middle school teachers. It would be easier if students' prior experiences consisted primarily of understanding the meaning of fractions and reasoning about operations with whole numbers. But most students are taught traditional algorithms for fraction operations in elementary school without a solid foundation of conceptual understanding, and by the time they reach middle school, many of them have the rules all mixed up—and no sense of the reasonableness of their answers. The procedures they have been taught become obstacles, rather than supports, to their understanding. "[Students] learn procedures by imitating and practicing them, and it is hard to go back and understand a procedure after you have practiced it many times" (Hiebert et al. 1997, 25). Other research (Pesek and Kirschner 2002) indicates that early instrumental instruction—"learning rules without reasons"— can interfere with subsequent attempts at relational learning—"knowing what to do and why" (Skemp 1978). Division of fractions, in particular, is one of the most rote procedures ("Ours is not to reason why—just invert and multiply!") in arithmetic instruction. Students easily confuse the series of steps for correct calculations, and they rarely have the opportunity to think about whether their answers are reasonable, what contexts call for division of fractions, or why invert-and-multiply makes sense.

The students in my class were fortunate to have spent sixth grade with a teacher who emphasized conceptual understanding of fractions and the use of benchmarks to estimate sums and differences. They also had practiced paper-and-pencil algorithms for addition, subtraction, and multiplication of fractions. Still, I approached the teaching of division with some trepidation. I had given a pre-assessment at the beginning of the year and knew that only Amy, Cheryl, Pirmin, and Iok could divide fractions accurately. But did they know why the procedures they used made sense? Just as in any class, the students had a wide variety of understandings and differing levels of competence with calculation, so I needed to figure out a way to make use of these differences so that the work we would do would engage and challenge everyone.

I thought about how our prior work might support this effort. We had just finished a unit on similarity in which students had examined the relationship between multiplication and division through the concept of scale factor. Fractional scale factors provided a context for and practice with multiplication by fractions, which is foundational knowledge for division. The students also had multiplied mixed numbers mentally using a variety of strategies, including the distributive property, rounding up and compensating, and the traditional algorithm. So at the time we began division, students had an intuitive sense about the impact of multiplication upon a fractional quantity.

Another consideration was a problem that had gradually emerged in our classroom discourse. A handful of students had begun to dominate the conversations, and discussions were often short-lived. While there were a few students (Christine, Sam, and Kara, especially) who were willing to say that they did not understand, subtle messages led me to believe that their status in the class was suffering. Somehow I needed to build a classroom environment where mistakes or wrong answers were seen as useful. I wasn't "trying to put a good face on a bad situation" (Hiebert et al. 1997, 48) but rather wanted to make purposeful use of their errors so everyone would learn more mathematics. This would be an important classroom norm to enact while studying division of fractions, which lends itself to right or wrong answers and which is heavily impacted by prior experiences and learning.

To accomplish this, I had recently tried a new strategy for our classroom discourse, "convince yourself, convince a friend, convince an enemy," adapted from *Thinking Mathematically* (Mason, Burton, and Stacey 1982, 95). While this technique is intended to subject one's own mathematical problem solving to increasing levels of scrutiny, I began to use it in classroom discussions in order to shift the emphasis from whether an *answer* was correct to whether an *explanation* was clear and convincing. This way, I hoped, students who did not understand something could place the burden on whoever was explaining (including me) to do so clearly. This emphasis on justification had the potential to foster all students' capacities for giving and analyzing logical arguments while at the same time building conceptual understanding of mathematical content. When I first introduced this procedure to the class, I replaced *enemy* with *skeptic* because of the literal minds of middle school students; we then practiced being skeptics with two problems. It seemed somewhat artificial at first, but soon this strategy became part of our collective vocabulary and practice.

My first priority in teaching division of fractions was to help students develop an intuition for what division by a fraction *means*. In order to bolster my own understanding of division by fractions, I read "Generating Representation: Division of Fractions" in *Knowing and Teaching Elementary Mathematics* (Ma 1999, 55–83), which focuses on different models for division of fractions. I also read "How Children Think About Division with Fractions" (Warrington 1997), which describes a fifth-grade teacher's experiences in building conceptual understanding of fraction division. Together, these readings helped me map out the terrain of the unit we would be studying.

I decided to begin our unit by following the progression in the Warrington article, outlined in the following section. While the disadvantage to this approach was that the initial problems would be decontextualized (what I call *naked number* problems), I thought it would be a useful way to assess how students thought about both fractions and division. After this initial assessment, I would be better equipped to decide how students should encounter problems that represented the different models for division of fractions. I would also have students investigate the traditional algorithm and see if they could justify each step; this would help them understand the use of properties in algebra and foster their reasoning skills. I anticipated their procedural fluency would develop through these experiences as well as through additional practice.

Prior to the Video Selection

I began the lesson by talking to the students about how we were going to study division of fractions. I make a habit of talking to my students about what we are going to do and why; this is part of the culture that explaining why we do things is something we do, whether it is about mathematics or my teaching decisions (Lampert 2001, 60). I told them that I knew they had studied addition, subtraction, and multiplication, but not division, of fractions in sixth grade, acknowledging that some of them had learned how to divide fractions at home or in other classes. I talked about how one of my goals for that day was to learn what they understood about division, not just what they could *do*. I told them that I was going to give them a series of problems to think about, and for each problem I wanted them to do two things (I put this on an overhead transparency):

- Decide without paper and pencil what you think the answer is.
- Try to prove that your answer makes sense.

The first problem I put up was $4 \div 2$. Immediately there was a smiling sound throughout the room. By this time in the year, the students trusted that I respected their mathematical competence; they also respected their own competence, and they knew that if I gave them a problem like this, I had a good reason. This relationship, built throughout the year, enabled them to be good-natured in addressing what to them must have looked like third-grade work.

The first fraction problem I gave was $6 \div \frac{1}{2}$. I made a deliberate decision to get the correct answer out of the way because the problem itself was a kind of setup: equating division by one-half with division by two is such a common misconception, even among the general public, that I knew a lot of students would think three was the answer without really thinking about it. So instead of taking the time for them to *discuss* what the answer was, I said, "First of all, what *is* the answer?" About half of the students raised their hands, and when I immediately said, "Not three," a lot of hands went down. (I don't know if I would do this again; I am curious to think about what would have happened if I had let them argue about the answer. The meaning of division by fractions may have been more transparent in this problem than in a more difficult one.) A few hands were still up, so I called on Amy, who said, "Twelve," and immediately a lot of kids said, "Oh!" I asked why this made sense, and as students started thinking about this, several of them raised their hands. I decided to call on Jordan, who seemed eager to talk.

Jordan offered to go to the board and use pictures to show why the answer was twelve. He wrote $\frac{1}{2}$ twelve times and said that each of the $\frac{1}{2}$s was a different "group-thingy" and "if you added up all of these [one-halves], you would get six." Since he had said the word "group" I figured he was thinking about division in terms of a measurement model. He then put plus signs between all of the $\frac{1}{2}$s and wrote $= 6$. By showing that there were twelve groups of one-half in six, Jordan was thinking about division as the number of groups of a certain size (in this case, the size was one-half) that could be removed from or were in a given quantity, which is how the class had interpreted $4 \div 2$. This also showed that twelve was the correct answer. I wondered, though, if the other students saw a connection between what he had written and the original problem, so I asked, "Why does that show that $6 \div \frac{1}{2} = 12$?" I didn't intend to put Jordan on the spot, but as soon as I asked, it felt like I had done just that.

Jordan turned back to look at what he had written and quickly said, "I don't know." I don't think Jordan understood my question; I think he felt he'd already explained his idea. I then asked the class to "help out" with the explanation, hoping that others would be able to interpret what Jordan had done as division.

Alicia helped out by saying that there were "twelve one-half parts going into six." I asked Jordan and Alicia how they would write it another way as a number sentence, and Jordan suggested, $12 \times \frac{1}{2} = 6$. Victor added $12/2 = 6$, which made me think he understood that multiplying by one-half and dividing by two were the same thing; and then Jessie contributed that the reciprocal of one-half times 6 was 12, which made me think he was employing the traditional algorithm. All of these ideas made a stew of representations that I doubted were being followed and understood by many of the students. I could have stopped at that point and made connections among the representations and shown how they fit with the original problem. But then Evan offered another way to think about it, going to the board and drawing a number line from 0 to 6 with $\frac{1}{2}$-length intervals marked. He showed that there were $12 \frac{1}{2}$-length intervals in the distance from 0 to 6. This representation made division by $\frac{1}{2}$ accessible visually and geometrically, even if it was only of the measurement model, and I felt ready to move on.

The next problem, $1 \div \frac{1}{3}$, was easy for students to visualize using Jordan's and Evan's methods; Ariel said that just like there were twelve halves in six, there were three one-thirds in one. The students all seemed to think about division this way and I was expecting that they would continue to use the same reasoning with the next problem ($1 \div \frac{2}{3}$). And, since the goal of this particular lesson was to learn how the students were thinking about fractions and division, I deliberately did not offer different models as new ways to think about division by fractions.

Watch "Defending Reasonableness: Division of Fractions," CD 1

Lesson Analysis and Reflection

After I posed $1 \div \frac{2}{3}$, most students became actively involved, so I knew that this was an appropriate task to discuss. Now I had to decide how to orchestrate the whole-class discussion. Sometimes I am selective about whom to call on in order to create a somewhat sequential path through a whole-class discussion, but at this moment I was not aware enough of the different ways people were thinking to do so. I called on Leslie, primarily because we had not heard from her recently. When she said, "Six," I was thankful this wrong answer had emerged because of its potential for a useful discussion. I have found the value of wrong answers to be inestimable as sites for learning in mathematics. Children's errors frequently have a logic that is based on misconceptions or a misapplication of rules they have previously been taught. As often as I can, I try to exploit these ideas to dig into the thorny issues that arise when thirty students are trying to understand mathematics from their own unique experiences and perspectives.

I also remembered that six was the same answer that Warrington's students had initially given, and I was curious about the logic behind it. Hoping we were onto something interesting, I said to Leslie, "And you think it is six because . . . " I noticed that her explanation (one-third goes into one three times, and two times three equals six) was largely procedural; I wondered why she multiplied two times three, but in the kind of split-second decision making that teachers deal with every day, I decided that before we examined this more closely it would be good to get some other ideas into the public arena. When Claire said she got one and a half (the right answer) because she switched the numerator and denominator, I used her explanation to send a strong message to the students about how important it was that they make sense of the problem rather than just follow a rule. I knew there would be plenty of opportunities for them to practice using the traditional algorithm or other algorithms for division, but today I wanted them to bring reasoning to whatever they were doing. So instead of explaining which of the two answers was correct, and because there were a lot of hands up in the room, I decided to have the students discuss in their groups what made sense to them.

I sometimes grapple with this idea of making sense. What am I really asking when I ask students to say why something makes sense? Is knowing that something makes sense the same thing as knowing why it works? It could make sense to them because it gets the right answer or because it is the way they were taught to do something. The belief, cultivated through years of experience in school, that math is all about following rules correctly is stubbornly resistant to change. For these students, "mathematics is never supposed to be a situation in which 'you don't know what to do.' If the teacher has done his or her job and the students have done their job, they should always be able to apply a fact, rule or procedure to obtain an answer quickly" (Frank 1988, 33). Moving from following rules to relying on their own mathematical reasoning can be a hard transition for many students to make at eleven or twelve years old—and one that some never do. We had worked hard all year on building sense making as a value in our class, however, and most of the students had been able to make this transition—some with resistance but many with explicit gratitude.

When Leslie had said six, I first thought that most students would disagree, but as I moved from group to group, I realized with surprise how many students thought six was correct! These small-group discussions serve several purposes for me. First, they give more students a chance to explain their thinking. Since I believe that the very process of explanation helps clarify thinking and solidify learning, I feel these discussions give more students an opportunity to learn. Second, small-group discussions are a valuable way for me to understand what students are thinking. "Eavesdropping" on their conversations is a powerful assessment tool that allows me to make better decisions about what the thrust of a whole-class discussion should be.

As I continued to walk around the classroom, I noticed that Sam had a pictorial model that was different from anything I had seen so far; I quietly asked him if he would be willing to share it later with the class. Then, when I sensed that the groups had exhausted what they could productively say to each other, I decided to start the whole-class discussion with Sam's idea. He carefully presented his pie chart model to justify the answer one and a half. Although it wasn't completely clear to me why he had drawn two circles, I guessed that his first circle was meant to define what $\frac{2}{3}$ was, while his second circle was to show how many of those two-thirds would fit into the same size whole. This explanation, while it was somewhat incomplete, contained nuggets that I thought could move the discussion along. I reminded the students about our "convince yourself, convince a friend, convince a skeptic" strategy and how we should use it in this discussion. I thought this would keep the focus of the lesson on sufficient justification and away from a polarization of who thought the answer was six and who thought it was one and a half.

Michael, in the role of a mathematical friend, was the first to comment on Sam's method, saying she had used the same reasoning to convince the skeptics in her group. I was pleased that Michael gave Sam credit for a good method; building on and giving credit to other people's thinking is one of the norms we had been working on since the beginning of the year. Then Ben, as a skeptic in Michael's group, was able to explain in his own words why one and a half made sense, and his thinking matched Sam's measurement model. It didn't matter that Ben really had thought the answer was six; being able to act as a skeptic had given him a role to play in the service of greater understanding. Then Evan said he agreed with Sam, Michael, and Ben but with a different reasoning—a linear model (what he called the "line way")—giving the class another way to visualize the division. He ran into a little trouble representing "one-third is half of two-thirds" arithmetically but got some help from Cheryl. And Cheryl, who thinks numerically much more readily than visually, then used the relationship between multiplication and division to justify the answer of one and a half. With all of these justifications, the students had many ways to think about division by two-thirds, and the case for one and a half as the correct answer was getting stronger and stronger.

But then Christine took the extraordinary step of admitting that she still thought the answer was six. This demonstrated a level of courage that few students could have summoned in the face of so much conflicting evidence. When she went to the board, her explanation was full of errors: she multiplied three by two, and then multiplied that by one. It appeared that her whole explanation was based on thinking that the problem was $1 \times (2 \times 3)$. Did this mean that she thought the division sign meant multiplication? It sure looked like it. And how had her classmates' arguments impacted her thinking? It appeared to me that she hadn't been able to make use of those arguments, as she did not even refer to them in her explanation. Watching Christine in class, and later reviewing her explanation on videotape, reminded me of one of my favorite quotations about arithmetic:

> The depressing thing about arithmetic badly taught is that it destroys a child's intellect, and, to some extent, his integrity. Before they are taught arithmetic, children will not give their assent to utter nonsense; afterwards, they will. (Sawyer in Burns 1994, 119)

For Christine, it appeared that making sense meant applying a rule that she thought she should follow. So instead of pressing her further, I asked Leslie what she thought now. It is unusual for me to call on students unless they volunteer, but I thought I was safe with Leslie, who had already discussed her ideas. There are disadvantages to calling primarily on volunteers, but my desire to avoid putting children on the spot currently dominates my practice.

Leslie didn't seem to mind being called on, and she readily responded that she had thought the answer was six but now she didn't think it "could be that big." Leslie was demonstrating that she could make use of the other students' arguments, that she could change her mind, and, most importantly, that she had begun to think about the *quantity* that the problem represented. Lampert says, "One of the hardest things to do in front of a group of one's peers is to make a mistake, admit one has made it, and correct it. Yet such a series of actions is an essential component of academic character" (2001, 266). Leslie did so with grace, and I secretly thanked her for her contribution to our collective learning. I then tried to bring Christine back into the conversation. She was willing to talk about how she had tried to employ Cheryl's method to help her make sense of the problem with numbers. Cheryl and Amy, in the meantime, were wildly bidding for attention. Amy argued that it couldn't be six, since "if you multiply six by two-thirds, it wouldn't equal one." Amy was showing a contradiction based on the relationship between multiplication and division: if $1 \div \frac{2}{3} = 6$, then $6 \times \frac{2}{3} = 1$. But since $6 \times \frac{2}{3} \neq 1$, then $1 \div \frac{2}{3} \neq 6$. Cheryl argued that Christine had misinterpreted the symbol for division.

With all of these ideas on the table, there were many teaching moves I could have made. Amy's argument was very sophisticated, and I could have moved the class discussion to a more abstract level by examining it more closely. I could have had a more detailed examination of Cheryl's use of inverse operations. I could have reiterated all of the arguments that had been presented so far.

But I decided instead to cut the conversation off in order to shine a brighter light on Leslie's idea that six was "too big" to be a reasonable answer. In order to do this, I quickly decided to bring context into the discussion but then had a hard time deciding what context to use! I knew I should choose the measurement model since that is how most students had been thinking about division so far. In retrospect, I also could have used the product and factors method since we had just finished working on multiplication (e.g., if the area of a rectangle is 1 square unit, and one of the sides is $\frac{2}{3}$ of a unit, what is the length of the other side?). Somehow the idea of lumber came into my mind. Here is a case where I wish I had been prepared with an example ahead of time; when I look at the example of lumber, it is rather embarrassing! In any event, lumber was the only thing I could think of, and I did not want students to leave class that day thinking that the answer could be six. I was surprised that the class discussion itself had not accomplished this, but I was ready to shift my role to contribute an argument. Inherent in the weight of my status as a teacher is the danger that students will disregard the often equally reasonable arguments of their peers. My desire to have students publicly share their thinking is not a perfunctory way of going through the motions before presenting the *real* way. But it was time to move on; reasonableness of quantity was my focus, and lumber was the only thing I could think of at the moment. As it turned out, the lumber example gave Christine access to the problem through the conversion of feet to inches, and I ended the lesson by saying, "One and a half is the correct answer."

In reflecting back over the whole lesson and reviewing the video yet again, I am left with many questions. The trouble with teaching is that there are so many paths to take, each with different results! I wonder if the conversation was worthwhile for everyone; I see Jessie and Iok in the foreground, for example, with little apparent interest in what else is going on in the class for much of the class period. While many in the class were active participants that day, I missed an opportunity to hear from each student by having them, at some point in the middle of the controversy, write about what they thought the answer was and why. I could also have asked them to write about what they had learned that day, a technique I often employ. I wonder what the students would have said.

Case Commentary—Jo's Analysis

Daniel Chazan and Deborah Ball (1999) wrote with some apparent frustration about the advice given in some mathematics education reform documents to "not tell" in the classroom. They illustrated, with examples from their own teaching, the different ways they needed to guide student discussions in order to make them productive. It was not a case of simply telling or not telling, but of drawing upon important pedagogical practices. These included "inserting substantive mathematical comments. We hold this to be a kind of 'telling,' a providing of intellectual resources, a steering, an offering of something intended both to contribute to and shape the discussion" (8). The act of managing a productive class discussion is extremely complicated and it involves a range of important and subtle pedagogical moves (Staples 2004). It is no wonder that many mathematics teachers steer away from such discussions, as the orchestration of a class discussion is difficult and many teachers have simply not had the opportunity to learn the different pedagogical practices they may need to do it well. In this case of teaching we saw a highly productive discussion that the teacher was not expecting. The students in the case entered into a mathematical disagreement regarding the answer to the question—what is one divided by two-thirds? Cathy wanted the students to review previously learned material, engaging in different acts of representation to illustrate and justify their answers; she did not expect a student to give the answer six and was even more surprised by the number of students concurring with that answer. In the events that followed, we saw some important learning taking place as students realized that the answer of six did not make sense. The students were convinced by the different representations they saw and the conversation appeared to flow smoothly. It is possible to watch such cases of teaching and think that the teacher is doing relatively little in the moment, concluding that the students are self-motivated or the teacher has done all of the work in the past, establishing careful classroom norms (Yackel and Cobb 1996; Kazemi 1998). A range of important norms supported the discussion, but a careful viewing of the case reveals that Cathy enacted a number of pedagogical practices that enabled the conversation to flow. I will review a selection of these now.

Requiring Students to Be Skeptical

One of the most important moves that a teacher can make is to ask students to play the role of skeptics, as Cathy has described in her writing. This simple act changes the entire nature of the classroom environment, as students no longer have to fear the shadow that hangs over many mathematics classrooms—that of being wrong. If some students appear to know something, others are asked to be skeptical. Whether the listeners understand or not, they are told to push their peers to give clear and vivid explanations, to demand high standards of evidence and alternative representations. This move shifts the emphasis from being confused or wrong to requiring evidence and justification. If students do not understand something, they do not have to declare their lack of understanding; instead they can say that insufficient evidence has been given, requiring the speaker to explain in different or better ways. We saw this clearly when Michael told us that Ben was the skeptic in their group, and later Ben explained how he became convinced that the answer was indeed one and a half, having previously thought it was six. This pedagogical move may be a helpful resource for teachers who want students to offer their ideas without fear of being incorrect and who would like high standards of representation and justification in their classroom.

The requirement that students play the part of skeptics has another important impact on the events in the classroom, because it shifts the role of the audience in the class. In many classrooms students are asked to present their answers to questions, but they are usually asked to do so only when they have correct answers. The role for other students in such instances is relatively passive—they are just listening to learn the correct answer, so those who believe they already know the answer will be likely to tune out. In Cathy's classroom, students are not asked to present their answers; they are asked to show representations of their ideas and to justify why they make sense. None of the audience members will have the same exact answer, and all the students have a role—to decide whether the representation and justification are sufficiently convincing for them. This gives the other students in the class a more active role than is typical, and the levels of interest and engagement are consequently higher than those I see in many classrooms when students are presenting.

Some readers may worry that the students in the case who offered the answer six were put on the spot and embarrassed by the conversation. Some months after the conversation had taken place, I interviewed students who had been involved in the debate, including Leslie and Christine (see video interviews on CD 2). The students were extremely forthcoming about the lesson and the mathematics approach more generally. Leslie and Christine, who had offered the answer six, said that they were not embarrassed, because they knew that it was all right to be wrong and that wrong answers played a productive role in the classroom. They were also able to demonstrate a good understanding of one divided by two-thirds, with one of the students drawing upon Cathy's lumber example, which she said helped her visualize the answer. Students also told me that they had enjoyed mathematics for the first time that year because they were able to discuss their ideas. They talked about learning from wrong answers and how they "wouldn't learn it from someone just explaining the right answer." They also told me that they were more confident using mathematics without a calculator and they now understood algorithms and rules such as "invert and multiply." The students communicated a number of interesting ideas, and two of the interviews are included on CD 2.

Communicating Interest in Student Ideas

Cathy set up a debate between students with different answers by saying, "Excuse me, this is really interesting. The side of the room I talked to, about half of the people thought it was six and about half the people thought it was one and a half."

This communicated the teacher's interest in the different answers and set the stage for the students to have a discussion in which they needed to give convincing mathematical arguments. Cathy legitimated both answers, not for their mathematical correctness (she asks in the clip, "Is this the kind of problem you can have two different answers to?"), but for their role in learning. She also communicated an interest in the discussion that would take place and the different arguments that students could give to support their thinking. Of course the quality of the discussion rested not only upon Cathy's words in setting up the debate but on a range of classroom norms (Yackel and Cobb 1996), including having respect for different answers; providing justification; representing ideas (we saw a number of well-chosen and crafted representations on the board); and making sense of answers.

Measuring Individual Understanding

Cathy collected two answers to the problem and asked the students which made sense. She then looked around the room for "hands up" to see who was able to offer an argument. She followed this with "OK, I've got almost one hand in every group but not quite. I want every group to come up with what makes sense." This communicated an aspect of Cathy's teaching that is evident in different cases; her simultaneous attention to the needs of the class and the needs of individuals. At that moment Cathy could probably have heard a number of explanations and had a class discussion around them, but she wanted to make sure that all the individuals in the class had experienced the opportunity to think carefully about the problem. The fact that not every group had at least one volunteer was a measure that told Cathy the students needed more time to think. Teaching is a constant act of navigation between attending to the needs of individuals and attending to those of the whole class (Lampert 2001), an issue that Cathy addresses through this pedagogical move.

Having Students Support Each Other at the Board

When a student struggled to explain something at the board, Cathy asked him if he would like to call on someone to help him, an offer that he happily accepted. This relieved the tension that can so easily be created when a student is required to think publicly. It also showed that Cathy sees mathematical work as a collective enterprise. I always remember a lesson I was watching in England when a teacher asked a girl to come to the board to present something and the girl replied that she had worked jointly with her partner and she did not want to explain alone. The teacher was rather taken aback but agreed to let both students come to the board. This changed the nature of classroom presentations and from that point on, students always presented jointly and felt much more confident doing so.

Hold That Thought!

A move of particular interest to me that can be seen in the teaching extract came about when a student offered an idea that was not one that Cathy thought would help the class at that time. This happened when Cheryl offered an explanation for the division problem using the inverse of fractions. Cathy asked the class why it made sense and Christine answered "I don't really understand, like, I still think it's six because . . . "

Cathy stopped Christine, saying, "Oh wait, Christine. And I know you've had your hand up and I want to call on you about why it's six but just, what method is Cheryl using here for this one?" Cathy knew that Christine needed to talk, but she also knew that Cheryl's method required some unpacking. These are the types of competing demands that teachers navigate between all the time (Lampert 1985). Less experienced teachers may have let Christine continue speaking, but Cathy knew she could employ a pedagogical practice of asking Christine to wait. Along with following the directive "not to tell," some teachers may also think that they should accept every student contribution to a discussion. Asking a student to hold her thought is an important pedagogical move that allows the teacher to respect a student's thinking and at the same time maintain an important mathematical direction. The teacher respects the students contribution (and ultimately returns to her idea), but allows the conversation to keep its mathematical thread.

Encouraging Student Presentations

In the middle of the clip, Cathy privately asked Sam if he would be willing to go to the board and "draw a picture" in order to "make an argument." At other times students volunteered to show their representations and arguments on the board. On some occasions Cathy asks a student to offer his thinking and yet other times she tells students in advance that one of them will be the reporter for their group. In this case Cathy asked a student to show his work because she thought his representation was particularly interesting and would communicate something important to the class. These are all different ways that Cathy encourages students to participate in the discussion, and all of these pedagogical moves are valuable aspects of her repertoire. In the case that accompanies Chapter 7, we'll see a class discussion about participation. Different students shared their thoughts about the methods teachers use to encourage participation and how they felt about them. The encouragement of participation is an important part of a teacher's work and it is helpful to examine different methods by which experienced teachers do so.

Choosing to Curtail the Discussion

The end of the video showed Cathy telling the students about a situation that could involve the problem $1 \div \frac{2}{3}$: a piece of lumber being divided into sections.

She chose to curtail the conversation in order to give it closure. One of the most difficult decisions teachers have to make when they have classroom discussions is when to end them—when have students discussed something enough? One of the major constraints in such a decision is that of time, teachers' most limited and precious resource. Teachers have to balance the desire for having students talk and formulate their ideas with the need to end the lesson or move to a new activity. This is one example of a closing point, which Cathy chose to mark with a particular contextual illustration. Suzanne Wilson describes teaching as an act of producing "metaphors, analogies, simulations, visual representations, explanations, models and a host of other representations that communicate aspects of the subject matter" (1992, 66). Cathy wrote in her reflection that she is now embarrassed by the example she chose, although the representation seems well chosen and appears to have illustrated division of fractions well. Christine (who was resilient in her thinking that the answer was six) referred to this example in an interview some months later, saying that the representation had given her an understanding of the correct process and answer. The connection between the mathematical method and the particular example from the world provided additional insights for the students.

The Devil Is in the Details

This case revealed a selection of different pedagogical moves that were employed in the service of learning. Each move is important and demonstrates the complexity of a teacher's work. Such moves also demonstrate the level, or "grain size," at which teaching decisions are made. Teachers are often offered advice that is at a much bigger grain size, such as whether to use group work to have discussions or lecture. We see from this and other lessons that teachers need to make decisions that are at a smaller grain size, such as when and how to curtail a discussion, which examples of representation to use, or which students to call upon. The field of educational research has not developed extensive knowledge of the detailed pedagogical practices that are helpful for teachers to learn, yet the difference between effective and ineffective teaching probably rests in the details of moment-to-moment decision making.

For an interesting look at students' reflections on this lesson, please see Reflections on the Fraction Discussion, on CD 2. In the interview, I play the video of the fraction discussion for three of the students who were involved in it (Christine, Leslie, and Ben) and ask them to reflect upon it.

Chapter 5

Introducing the Notion of Proof
(May 15)

Justification is central to mathematics, and even young
children cannot learn mathematics with understanding without
engaging in justification.

CARPENTER, FRANKE, AND LEVI (2003, 85)

Instructional programs from prekindergarten through grade 12 should
enable all students to—
- *recognize reasoning and proof as fundamental aspects of*
  mathematics;
- *make and investigate mathematical conjectures;*
- *develop and evaluate mathematical arguments and proofs;*
- *select and use various types of reasoning and methods of proof.*

NCTM (2000, 262)

Background of the Lesson—Cathy's Perspective

The class had just taken the final test on an algebraic reasoning unit that had begun with the Border Problem (see Chapters 2 and 3). While one focus of this unit had been on the multiple representations of functions (e.g., tables, graphs, algebraic expressions, verbal descriptions), an important emphasis had been on having students express algebraically what they had visualized geometrically. This meant that several different equivalent expressions emerged from the students for any given problem. For example, in the problem seen in Figure 5–1 (a growth pattern that is assumed to continue indefinitely in the same manner), the students had generated four different expressions to relate the stage number (n) to the number of tiles.

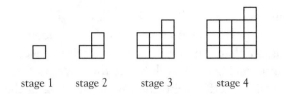

stage 1
stage 2
stage 3
stage 4

Figure 5–1.

$$n \cdot (n-1) + 1$$
$$n^2 - n + 1$$
$$n^2 - (n-1)$$
$$n + (n-1)(n-1)$$

They had learned to justify the validity of their algebraic expressions geometrically, as shown in Figures 5–2 through 5–5.

Through these geometric representations, I had helped the students understand that their algebraic expressions were equivalent, but I had chosen not to

n·(n-1)+1
□+1
n-1
n

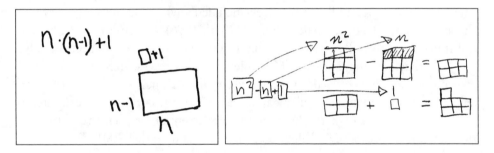

Figure 5–2. This justifies $n \cdot (n-1) + 1$.

n²
n
n²-n+1
1

Figure 5–3. This justifies $n^2 - n + 1$.

n=stage #
n²–(n-1)
1
n-1
n
n

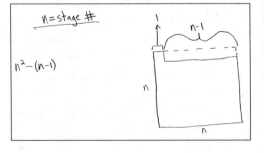

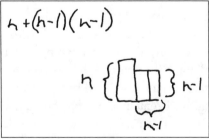

Figure 5–4. This justifies $n^2 - (n-1)$.

n+(n-1)(n-1)
n
n-1
n-1

Figure 5–5. This justifies $n + (n-1)(n-1)$.

teach algebraic methods for simplifying them. Besides the fact that our curriculum did not include applying the distributive property to symbolic expressions or multiplying binomials, another important consideration influenced this decision. I was concerned that introducing these skills before the students' fragile understandings had taken root would interfere with their understanding of the concepts (Pesek and Kirschner 2000). My priority in the unit had been for students to learn how to generate and use algebraic expressions to represent relationships that the students themselves had observed. Simplifying those expressions, a somewhat trivial skill, would result in stripping the expressions of meaning and connections with geometry, whereas maintaining the original form of those expressions helped give meaning to the language of algebra. And, because their geometric explanations were convincing to themselves and others, my students were coming to understand they did not need an external authority (me) to provide a stamp of approval to validate their thinking. The establishment of this intellectual autonomy was an important result of the work they had been doing.

At this time I had just finished the course work for my master's degree, and the centrality of proof to mathematics had been fully impressed upon me. For some years it had struck me as strange and worrisome that the long lists of mathematics standards in middle school rarely included anything akin to proof or other "habits of mind" (Cuoco, Goldenberg, and Mark 1996) so intrinsic to mathematical thinking. How will students be able to critically analyze situations or solve problems they have never seen before unless they learn to search for patterns, to conjecture, to prove? Indeed, in *Adding It Up,* the "capacity for logical thought, reflection, explanation, and justification" is described as one of five interconnected strands of mathematics learning that are essential for what the editors call "mathematical proficiency" (Kilpatrick, Swafford, and Findell 2001, 5).

We had established a class norm in which students consistently justified their thinking so that, as Hiebert (1997) say, "the authority for reasonability and correctness lies in the logic and structure of the subject" (9–10). And, as seen in Chapter 4, I had encouraged students to make arguments that would convince themselves as well as a (mathematical) friend and a skeptic (Mason, Burton, and Stacey 1982) in order to subject the validity of their thinking to increasing levels of scrutiny. But so far I had not given students the explicit opportunity to connect the justification they had been doing to the notion of proof in the more rigorous mathematical sense. Then, as I was writing the unit test, I saw an opportunity to do so. I remembered that one day early in the unit, Sarah had conjectured that $2(n - 1)$ was the same thing as $2n - 2$. Curious about how students would approach a proof of this conjecture without having any geometric context from which to build, I decided to include it as an extra-credit question on their unit test. I posed the problem this way: "A couple of weeks ago, there was a conjecture in our class that $2(n - 1) = 2n - 2$. Prove that this is true."

I knew students understood that $2(n-1)$ was another way of writing $2 \times (n-1)$, so notation would not be an obstacle to their thinking. They also had worked with parentheses in their practice with order of operations, and they had developed skill in substituting numerical values for the variables in expressions they had written; this would give them ready access to the problem numerically. I also thought students understood the distributive property numerically because of the mental arithmetic exercises in which we regularly engaged. For example, students made a habit of calculating 4×78 as $(4 \times 70) + (4 \times 8)$, or $3 \times 2\frac{3}{4}$ as $\left(3 \times 2\right) + \left(3 \times \frac{3}{4}\right)$. I had on several occasions told them that this process was an important mathematical property, called the distributive property of multiplication over addition. But students had had no experience with algebraic manipulations involving this property; indeed, if they had, then this extra-credit question would have been a procedural exercise with little cognitive demand. Because they lacked this formal experience, the question offered me an opportunity to assess students' notions of justification.

As I scored their tests, I became aware that although only about half of the students had attempted the extra-credit question, broad patterns were evident in the responses of those who did. Carpenter, Franke, and Levi (2003) observe, "Students' attempts to justify that mathematical statements are true can be separated into three broad classes: appeal to authority, justification by example, and generalizable arguments" (87). While none of my students appealed to authority, most students employed justification by example, satisfied that they had proven the conjecture by showing that the two expressions were equal for one particular value of n (a few students used two or more different values of n). Only a handful had tried to use a generalizable argument by using either words alone or words and pictures. I thought it was time to collectively consider the limits of justification by example, so I decided to engage everyone in a class discussion.

Prior to the Video Selection

On the day this discussion took place, I had handed back their tests and we had spent about half of the period going over the questions. The video selection begins as I direct their attention to the extra credit problem.

Watch "Introducing the Notion of Proof," CD 1

Lesson Analysis and Reflection

I was not certain how to orchestrate our collective journey into this as yet uncharted terrain. I knew I wanted to challenge the students to think about numbers in general and expose them to the notion of mathematical proof. But it was a journey we were going to take together. I would have to decide as we went along which ideas would move our path in productive directions.

I remembered that in an earlier lesson, Krysta had used a counterexample to prove that two expressions were *not* equivalent, so I wondered if some students might assume that using one example could prove that they *were* equivalent. I planned generally to have students think about why particular examples might not be sufficient and consider how one might prove that a statement was true for all numbers and then see what happened.

I started by demonstrating a correct substitution (six for the variable) in order to set the stage for the discussion and to make sure that everyone had access to the accurate arithmetic. As soon as I said, "Ten equals ten," Ana repeated what I had said and smiled—she thought I was joking. It struck me that Ana, among others, was still not used to the equals sign as a symbol of equivalence, but rather a "get the answer" operator. We often assume that students understand so much more than they do about important mathematical ideas such as equality. I filed this away for future consideration and plunged into the discussion I wanted to have with them.

My first question, "What's wrong?" gave students the clue that one example wasn't enough, and Sarah's response (that just because it worked for six didn't mean it would work for other numbers) sounded like the obvious answer. Were the other students beginning to wonder what else they would need to do? Was the process of proving $2(n - 1) = 2n - 2$ a trivial activity that didn't engage their curiosity? I didn't know yet.

Building on what Sarah had said, I wondered aloud if we should try another number. I wanted to get, and give the students, a sense of what others in the class thought were enough examples. In asking my next question ("How many numbers would you have to try before you were convinced that it would always work?"), I was hoping to raise a controversy that would challenge students to consider the idea that they could never use enough examples to be certain that the statement would always be true.

The impact of how questions are worded is so interesting! In retrospect, that particular question may have misled the students into thinking there might be some sufficient number, which certainly wasn't my intent. It also occurred to me—later—that being "convinced that it would always work" wasn't really the heart of what I was driving at. There is a big difference between being *convinced* that something works and *proving* that it does. When considering the truth of a mathematical statement, a couple of well-chosen examples may indeed convince us—or at least build our intuition about—whether it is true or not. But once we have decided that it is true, setting out to prove it is another thing entirely. I had asked my students about the first part but not the second! I later found another question that might have done a better job of capturing the students' imaginations and giving them a broader way to think about proving that something would always work: "Okay, so we have seen that it works for a lot of numbers, but how do we know that there is not some number—maybe a very, very big number—that it will not work for?" (Carpenter, Franke, and Levi 2003, 96). When I saw this question, I thought, "Why didn't *I* think of that?" That got me to thinking about other ways I might have challenged the students to think about numbers in general; for example, I could have asked, "Would this be true for fractions? Negative numbers?" All of these questions would have been interesting to pursue. Reflecting on the lesson in this way makes it so plain that teaching decisions, especially those made when enacting a lesson for the first time, are complicated and fraught with trial and error. It also makes me appreciate the importance of collaboration. I know that if I had discussed this lesson in depth with my colleagues before teaching it, I would have avoided some of the pitfalls that working in isolation almost guarantees.

The video clip gave us the opportunity to eavesdrop on Pam, Melissa, Colin, and Joey as the small-group discussions began. Pam and Melissa, who had attempted a general proof, using a picture, on her test, appeared to have immediately grasped the idea that if they could understand the general idea of this situation for one number, they would not need to try any other numbers. This is an important step toward thinking about numbers in general. Pam talked about making what she called a "generic genre" explanation like she had done for Rod Rafts. Pam was referring here to a recent problem in which students were to write an algebraic expression relating the number of Cuisenaire® Rods (built in the shape of a raft) to the surface area of the raft. An important part of their work had been to show, geometrically, why their algebraic expressions would always work, no matter how many rods were in the raft. I had used the word *general* to describe both their algebraic expressions and the geometric justifications that supported those expressions. The students had started calling them *generic* instead, but Pam's use of the word *genre* must have come from her English class!

As the groups of students talked, I did not spend as much time as I usually do wandering around the room, listening to their conversations. I noticed the animated conversation between Pam and her group from across the room but, of course, couldn't hear what they were saying. I assumed that most students would quickly agree that there was no magic number of examples that would prove a statement was true and hoped to spend the greater part of our remaining class time on how a general argument might be made. After a short time, I called the students back together to begin our class discussion. But I was in for a surprise.

I was determined to bring more boys' voices into the conversation that day. During the last few weeks I had noticed that a few students were doing most of the talking—all of them girls. While the class had many articulate and confident girls, the boys, outnumbered two to one, were generally quiet and somewhat shy. I think all students should share their ideas with the whole class at least some of the time for everyone's benefit. I read in *Making Sense*, "To the extent that some students are excluded and do not participate, the learning possibilities are diminished for everyone" (Hiebert et al. 1997, 67). I continue to juggle the competing priorities of making sure everyone's voice is heard and making sure no one is put on the spot. One way I have dealt with this is to have a student reporter share what his or her group discussed; this is based on the assumption (possibly erroneous; see Chapter 7) that reporting for one's group causes less anxiety than having to explain one's own ideas. I decided to use this strategy in that day's discussion.

I called on Colin first because I was curious about what his group had been talking about. As he spoke, though, I couldn't understand what he meant about using one number; when I pressed him, I realized he wasn't clear on it either. Rather than ask a different group member to help out, I decided to get thoughts from the other groups before pursuing this idea further.

When David reported for his group, I was amazed that all of those students still thought that some particular number of examples (three, five) would be convincing; maybe my question *had* been misleading and they were answering in good faith with a number? Then, when the second David reported that his group members would be convinced after some number of examples (less than ten because after that, "you [would] get the point"), I started to wonder if I should make a move to change the direction of the discussion.

In retrospect, I realize I need not have worried. So often in class discussions, if I am patient, students will raise the important ideas that need consideration; this responsibility is not mine, as the teacher, alone. On that day Travis introduced the important new idea, saying, "You would have to try every number there is . . . because maybe like one through thirty would work but it might not work for thirty-one . . . so you have to find some way to explain it in words." I was struck by his eloquence and thought it was important enough to pursue it in depth. This is another interesting part of orchestrating class discussions; while it is important to hear different ideas, all of the ideas will not have equal significance. Part of my job is to help the students find the important mathematics in the many ideas that emerge in a discussion. So, rather dramatically for emphasis, I asked Travis to repeat what he had said. He got a little flustered and had some trouble getting it out, and then the class laughed at the idea of having to try every number ("and there's a lot of them"). Sarah and Mindy, Travis' group members, tried to help by describing their perspectives. Mindy also had a lot of trouble putting her thoughts into words, but Sarah, after a little stumbling, was able to describe their idea; she explained that what was important was *how* it worked, not just *that* it worked for certain numbers. I think she meant that if she knew how it worked, she would be able to understand why it would work for any number.

At this point I had abandoned my well-planned selection of particular reporters, and Stephanie was eager to comment, so I called on her. She added to the layers of this conversation by referring to the Border Problem—the very first problem in our unit—and how they had been asked to explain why the formulas worked. She said this problem was the same: you would need to show *why* it worked. And when Melissa spoke, I realized what Colin had been trying to say earlier: that if you could understand and explain why it worked for one number, you wouldn't need to try any others. This would have been a great time to put the groups back to work to think about why it worked and to start to form a more general argument. But I had forgotten that we were on a short-day schedule and was so involved in what was emerging in the discussion that I had no idea what time it was. I was shocked to hear the bell ring—and determined to continue working on this problem the next day.

Case Commentary—Jo's Analysis

Offering Multiple Opportunities for Understanding

We saw in this case a strategy that I have seen Cathy employ often—that of asking groups to discuss something before having a class discussion. On this day the group discussion was very brief—only one minute long—and Colin was unable to reproduce the explanation he'd heard from his group. Cathy was later regretful that she had given the groups so little time and that she had put Colin on the spot, but the event created an opportunity for teacher learning, and Cathy was particularly intrigued and pleased to observe the interactions that occurred among group members that were captured on video. The event of note took place when Cathy asked students to discuss this question: "How many numbers would you have to try before you were convinced that it would always work?" The camera moved to a small group in which Colin, James, Pam, and Melissa discussed the question. Pam immediately launched into some sophisticated mathematical reasoning, explaining that one could understand why one number worked and then move to a more generic explanation, using, for example, generic blocks. She gave a rudimentary description of proof by generalization. Then something very interesting happened: Cathy called the class together and asked different group members to explain the discussions in their groups. The first person she called upon was a member of the group we watched in the video. Colin, who sat and nodded through Pam's explanation as though following what she was saying, attempted to repeat the explanation, but when Cathy pushed for elaboration, it was clear that he did not understand the idea.

Colin's response is interesting partly because it illustrates the difficulties of learning through being told. Cathy gave the groups only a very short time to discuss their responses and this group could clearly have benefited from having more time to discuss the ideas. In the short time they had, Colin was only able to hear Pam's idea and was unable to learn from it. When asked to report for his group, he could only repeat some words, and when pushed, he stalled completely. A wide body of research has shown that students do not learn simply by being told, they need to actively connect new knowledge with their previous conceptions and beliefs (Bransford, Brown, and Cocking 2000). In essence, we do not learn what people say, we learn from what they say (Schwartz 1999). There is something more active that takes place in the process of learning than just hearing words. This is the basic tenet of constructivism, the idea that learners need to construct understanding by making connections. However, teaching by telling remains a pervasive mode of instruction at all levels. Of course there are times when telling plays a critical role—an interesting lecture given at the right time, and designed to fit with students' current ideas and questions, can catapult understanding tremendously (Schwartz and Bransford 1998)—but telling should take its place alongside other modes of instruction, to complement and support them. When Cathy watched the tape of the small-group interaction, she realized that Colin needed other opportunities, such as discussing the ideas, drawing them, or making an argument from them, to make sense of the proposal he had heard.

Giving Emphasis to Important Ideas

Another pedagogical strategy that was salient in this case was that of dramatic emphasis. When Travis offered his idea that "just because it works for maybe twenty or thirty of them, maybe one through thirty would work, but it might not work for thirty-one," Cathy responded in two ways. First she paused dramatically, for a full seven seconds, before speaking. She also made a silent gesture telling students to lower their hands. The use of emphasis and accentuation makes a conversation more interesting. When groups discuss ideas there is more texture to the conversation than when a teacher talks for a long time, and students will often be more interested and pay more attention when different students talk and when they know they can contribute to ideas (Schwartz 1999), but teachers play an important role by giving emphasis to certain ideas and by mediating the contributions of different students. This is important "intellectual" work (Lampert 2001, 174) as it involves judging both the validity of different ideas and their usefulness in supporting the learning of others. One of the tasks of learning involves working out which ideas are more critical than others. In this moment Cathy communicated that Travis' idea was important and worth attending to and the students responded by listening carefully and by building upon Travis' contribution.

Reinforcing Classroom Norms

One of the actions Cathy enacted in this clip was to silently ask students to put their hands down. In the fraction case we also saw Cathy tell students—more strongly—to put their hands down. In the Border Problem case we heard her say, "I'm distracted, Wendy, by your hand being up right now. Please listen to Sarah!" Some viewers of the cases will take offense at this—after all, it is good to encourage students' contributions and to support rather than inhibit their participation. But Cathy was reinforcing an important norm—that of listening to other students (and the teacher). If hands start to shoot up as soon as a student starts speaking, she may think she has said something wrong or that her input isn't valued, which could make her very uncomfortable. Of course those who shoot their hands up are often engaged in a delightfully passionate way, but they may inhibit the involvement of more reticent students. Erikson talks about "turn sharks," those who jump into group conversations when someone falters or pauses, stepping in "at the smell of blood in the water" (1996, 37–38; Barron 2003). Turn sharks are dominant in small-group conversations, but students who shoot their hands in the air when someone else is speaking to the class are engaging in similar behavior. Cathy communicated the undesirability of this behavior to students, urging them to refrain from raising their hands until the speaker had finished.

Piquing Students' Interest

Some people have watched this case and criticized the question Cathy asked: "How many numbers would you have to try before you were convinced that it would always work?" They have said the wording suggests a numerical answer and is therefore a trick question. Indeed, the act of *convincing* using a mathematical argument is not the same as *proving*, and some people may be convinced by a selection of numbers, especially if they understand *why* they work, as Pam pointed out in her small-group discussion at the beginning of the clip. Others have told me that the discussion was not a good use of time, as it was five minutes at the end of class. I regard the five minutes to be time well spent, particularly because it was the end of class. Time is such a precious resource for teachers and yet I have often witnessed classes fizzling out in the last five minutes as students pack away their books and prepare to leave. In a number of the cases accompanying this book, we see students passionately engaged, continuing to think and debate even after the bell has sounded. In this way students learn that mathematical inquiry exists without boundaries, it cannot be crafted to begin and end within a single class period, nor can it be limited to the confines of a single classroom. Cathy teaches her students that mathematical discovery is an endeavor to be carried out of classrooms and into the world. Some debates, such as the one we saw in the fraction case, are important to end with closure; others may be left to brew for a while, especially if students' interest has been piqued. This is fortunate, given that teachers have the monumental task of bringing about intellectual growth, building upon students' ideas and interests, through a series of segmented class minutes that end abruptly each day with a bell! The discussion continued in the next class period, which can be viewed as part of our next case.

Chapter 6

Continuing Our Discussion of Proof
Convincing Others

In grades 6–8 students should sharpen and extend their reasoning skills by deepening their evaluations of their assertions and conjectures and using inductive and deductive reasoning to formulate mathematical arguments. They should expand the audience for their mathematical arguments beyond their teacher and their classmates. They need to develop compelling arguments with enough evidence to convince someone who is not part of their own learning community.

PSSM (2000, 262)

Background of the Lesson—Cathy's Perspective

The day before, our class had begun a discussion about how to show that $2(n - 1)$ and $2n - 2$ were equivalent expressions. Since we had not yet studied the distributive property with variables, most students were satisfied with substituting one or more numbers for n. During the discussion, however, Travis had pointed out that even if they tried lots of numbers, there might be some number that would not work "so you would have to find some way to explain it in words." I thought Travis, in saying this, was alluding to an emerging notion that words might achieve something that trying lots of examples couldn't—they could show *why* the expressions were equivalent. Sarah echoed Travis' thinking by saying that it wasn't enough to show *that* it worked—you needed to show *why* it worked. But the discussion was prematurely shortened by a special schedule that day, which I had forgotten. And, although disappointed, I was glad to have more time to think about how to continue the lesson.

After some thought, I decided to begin by summarizing Travis' idea. Then I wanted students to think about this question on their own: how would they prove to someone else that the statement $2(n-1) = 2n - 2$ was true for all numbers? I am learning to make a habit of having individual think time before getting small-group discussions started so that everyone has a chance to internalize the problem for him- or herself; this generally brings more students into the conversation and can increase the number of ways of thinking generated about any particular problem.

I also planned to structure the small-group discussions by having students share their ideas in a particular order. This would provide each student the opportunity and obligation to share his or her thinking and, in turn, to hear everyone else's ideas. Then I would have them share their thoughts in a whole-class discussion.

Watch "Continuing Our Discussion of Proof: Convincing Others," CD 1

Lesson Analysis and Reflection

I was eager for class to start so that I could find out what would happen, but as soon as I summarized Travis' idea I could tell that the students weren't nearly as interested in this as I was! Undeterred, I pressed on, trusting that their energy and interest would revive when they started working with their groups.

After the individual think time, I set the stage for their small-group discussions with a little talk reminding students how to respond to one another in these discussions. As Lampert (2001) says, "The work of establishing an environment in which students feel safe to do academic work with one another is a daily business requiring constant attention" (267). Behaviors like encouraging and showing people that you are listening have a big impact on the class culture, which in turn greatly influences how much students learn. It is easy, through inattention or neglect, to let students slip into careless and possibly negative behaviors that have adverse affects on learning. In the video clip, we indeed see Antony and Jose engaged in polite and largely productive discussion. Both boys made sense of the situation differently, although it is not clear that they were aware of this. Antony, using the relationship between addition and multiplication, saw $2(n-1)$ as $(n-1) + (n-1)$. He was confident as he explained why it made sense that the sum would be two ns and two minus ones.

Jose, attempting to follow Antony's reasoning, politely said, "That kind of makes sense." But the way he said this makes me think that he did not really understand at all. Teachers rarely have the luxury of being privy to small-group or partner conversations, and watching this interaction made me want to reemphasize to students that *pretending* that something makes sense, even for the sake of politeness, does not help anyone learn more. I had other questions after watching their interaction. Did Jose realize he didn't really understand Antony's explanation? If so, what would it have taken for him to be able to continue to press Antony until Jose really understood what Antony was saying? How was Jose's own way of thinking about it interfering with his ability to understand Antony's thinking?

Jose tried to rephrase what he thought Antony said, but he ended up expressing a somewhat different way of thinking about it (using multiplication and doubling and not mentioning addition at all). But it was then, when he described it his own way, that it sounded like he really did get it. But then Antony offended Jose by asking him if *he* had an idea, indicating that Anthony thought they both had the same method.

After some time, I called the class back together and asked for volunteers. When Colin raised his hand, I was glad that the previous day's experience (being called on and not being able to explain) did not discourage his participation that day. Colin gave a careful and clear (to me, at least) explanation and there were a lot of "Oh!"s. At this point, it might have been tempting to say, "Everyone got that?" or "Make sense?" and assume that, if no one protested, everyone was with Colin. As a teacher, it is appealing to think that once a correct mathematical idea has been stated, then everyone who has heard it has understood it, but this is generally wishful thinking. What seems crystal clear to one person (especially to the teacher) is often inaccessible to many others, and a question like "Does everybody understand that?" has only one correct answer—yes. In my experience, very few students have the intellectual courage to admit they don't understand when a majority of their peers say they do. The other hidden messages in a question like "Everyone got it?" are that understanding is an all-or-nothing proposition and that mathematical ideas have an "it" to get. Since "partially grasped ideas and periods of confusion are a natural part of the process of developing understanding" (California State Department of Education 1987, 14), I try to ask questions that seek to ferret out the complexity in mathematical ideas and explanations. For example, "*What* makes sense about Colin's explanation and what doesn't?" or "*Why* does that make sense?" would help to dispel the notion that understanding something is an all-or-nothing process.

Rather than have Colin sit down after his endearing bow, I asked him to remain and answer questions from his classmates, using "convince yourself, convince a friend, convince a skeptic" (Mason, Burton, and Stacey 1982) to keep the discussion afloat. This strategy (see also Chapter 4) helps place responsibility on the person who is explaining to make his explanations understandable and gives permission for anyone who doesn't understand *yet* to play the role of being unconvinced rather than being just slow to catch on.

Sure enough, when I asked if there were any skeptics, Stephanie immediately said, "I don't get it!" followed by Kay, whose explanation Colin readily endorsed.

Stephanie remained unconvinced, and she asked, "Where does the negative one come from?" What was interesting about her interaction with Colin was not only her persistence but the fact that her questioning led to an explanation that yielded even more "Oh!"s from the class than had his first explanation.

All this time I had been hoping that Melissa, who had used a diagram on the unit test, would volunteer to share this method with the class. When she didn't do so, I decided to ask her to share her thinking anyway because I wanted other students to see how a visual method could be used as a strategy for bringing sense to this problem. Although her (rather haphazard) diagram was based on a particular number (four), her proof was in fact a more general argument. She did not rely on the specific number four, but rather talked about it as n. And she did not simply calculate the answers—she never actually stated that both expressions were equal to six—saying instead that they were "the same thing." This kind of thinking was evidence of a move to a more general argument, in that her concrete solution provided a basis for generalization (Carpenter, Franke, and Levi 2003, 90).

At this point in the lesson, I did not see what would move the discussion along so that more learning would take place. While I thought that all of the students were convinced that $2(n - 1) = 2n - 2$ was true, their abilities to prove that it was true for all numbers appeared to be widely varied. I wanted to know what that variation looked like, so I decided to have each student write a justification. I knew that writing would serve as more, however, than an individual assessment for me. Writing, like doing mathematics, "requires gathering, organizing, and clarifying thoughts. It demands finding out what you know and what you don't know. It calls for thinking clearly" (Burns 1995, 3). Having the students write now would help them put their own thoughts into words and, in doing so, help them clarify their thinking.

Looking back at the lesson and examining the students' writing, it is clear that the students were spread across a broad continuum approaching the notion of a mathematical proof. Only a few students used what I would call truly general proofs; others used particular examples in a general way, and still others used only examples. The papers in Figures 6–1 through 6–3 give a sense of this continuum.

Surprisingly, several students still relied on proof by example, replacing n with particular numbers. A few students, however, used particular examples in a general way. For example David wrote, "I think $2(n - 1) = 2n - 2$ is true because they are the same equation, only different numbers are subtracted at different times." He then demonstrated this by drawing a 4-by-1 rectangle to represent n and showed how removing one square and then doubling the number of remaining squares would yield the same result as if he had first doubled n and then removed two squares. Although this seems almost the same as using one particular exam-

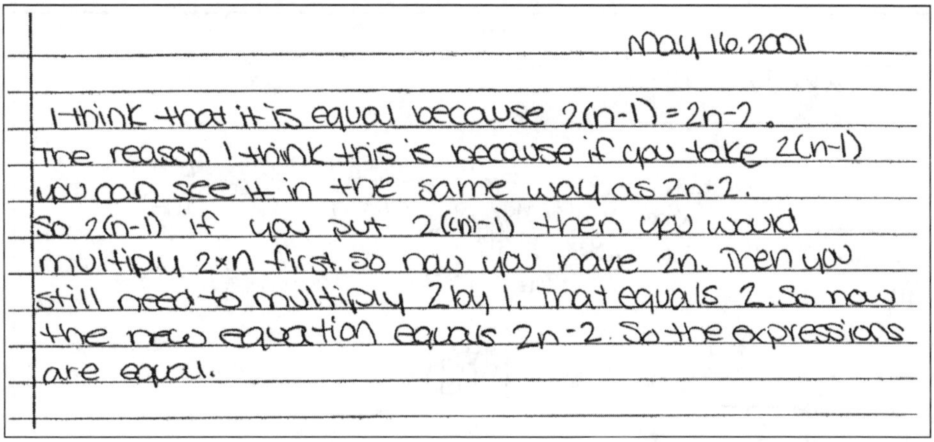

May 16, 2001

I think that it is equal because 2(n-1) = 2n-2.
The reason I think this is because if you take 2(n-1)
you can see it in the same way as 2n-2.
So 2(n-1) if you put 2(n-1) then you would
multiply 2×n first. So now you have 2n. Then you
still need to multiply 2 by 1. That equals 2. So now
the new equation equals 2n-2. So the expressions
are equal.

Figure 6–1.

ple (4 for *n*), David never stated that they both had six squares and the argument did not seem to depend on *n* being 4. Carpenter, Franke, and Levi (2003) describe this as "concrete examples that are more than examples" (89).

Other students employed what I would call a rule-following strategy that may actually be an appeal to authority, describing how to multiply across parentheses (see Figure 6–1). This is similar to the argument that might be made if one were familiar with applying the distributive property. But this particular student did something interesting that Carpenter, Franke, and Levi describe as restating the conjecture in an attempt to prove it (2003, 88). She wrote, "I think it is equal because $2(n-1) = 2n-2$. The reason I think this is because if you take $2(n-1)$ you can see it in the same way as $2n-2$."

The next student used a diagram similar to the one Melissa made on the board (see Figure 6–2). And even though this student drew a particular number of squares, there is no indication that the specific number of squares played any role in the proof. On the left is the diagram representing $2(n-1)$, where we see two separate but equal lengths, each with a –1 at the end. The diagram on the right shows the two lengths together as 2*n* with the –2 combined across the two lengths. This method could be applied to any number of squares and one could easily imagine the length as being *n*. This is closer to a general proof, limited only by the student's not knowing how to—or knowing that one could—draw a bar to represent any length.

The most general of the arguments was from the student whose work appears in Figure 6–3. This student, like Antony, understood $2(n-1)$ as two groups of

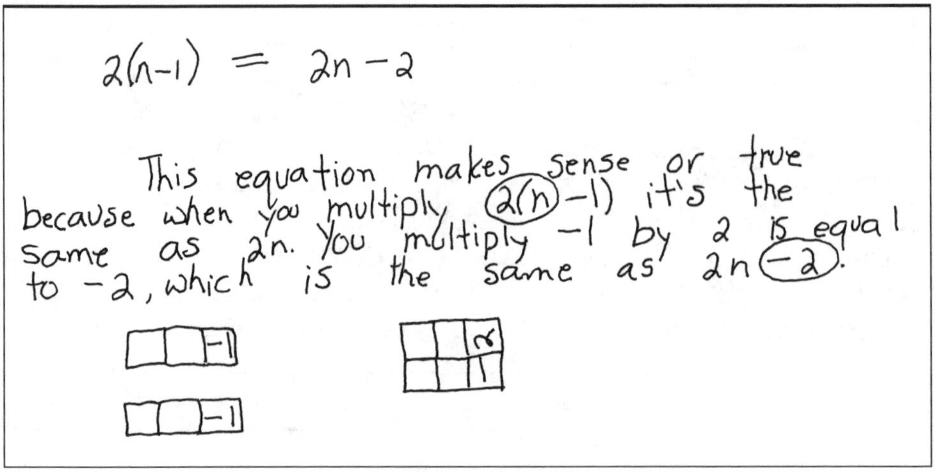

$$2(n-1) = 2n - 2$$

This equation makes sense or true because when you multiply (2(n)-1) it's the same as 2n. You multiply -1 by 2 is equal to -2, which is the same as 2n(-2).

Figure 6–2.

$$2(n-1) = 2n - 2$$

For 2(n-1) is just like (n-1)+(n-1). If you put them togethers It's like 2n-2. You can subtract 2 for the two minus ones. Instead of n+n, you can do 2·n or 2n.

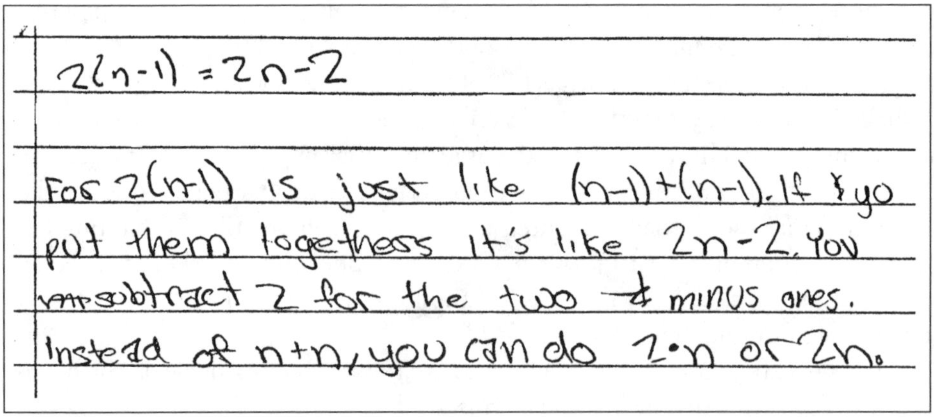

Figure 6–3.

$(n - 1)$, or $(n - 1) + (n - 1)$. The student then intuitively used the associative property to regroup the terms so that the "two minus ones" meant -2 and the $n + n$ meant $2n$. This explanation is elegant in its simplicity and clarity.

One of my colleagues wondered if spending a full class period on a skill that could be "taught" in five minutes was a good use of time. Reflecting on this comment, I thought that our valuable time was spent in much broader pursuits than on any one skill. Students constructed convincing arguments, thought about numbers in general, further developed their understanding of the language of algebra, and were initiated into a central practice of mathematicians. This to me is time well spent.

Case Commentary—Jos' Analysis

What was this lesson all about? Some would say that it was a lesson on mathematical proof; it began with Cathy reminding the class of Travis' claim that $2(n - 1)$ could not be *proved* to be the same as $2n - 2$ by substituting numbers. But the remainder of the lesson was not spent on discussions of proof, but on discussions and explorations of algebraic representation and equivalence. The majority of the students attempted to prove that the expressions were equivalent by manipulating the algebra and making sense of the changed expression. Some of the students were more familiar with the distributive property than others, so the task of manipulating the expression was differentially demanding for students, but everyone was required to make sense of the changed expression and to reason mathematically.

Quantitative Literacy

This lesson seems partly to be about the nature of mathematical proof and partly about the use of algebra in the *development* and representation of ideas. This lesson is also another example of the ways that Cathy's teaching promotes what may be thought of as *quantitative literacy* (Steen 1997). The notion of quantitative literacy has been developed both in response to an awareness that the general public finds mathematical work extremely difficult and in response to the realization that successful use of mathematics in life requires a different way of working than that generally taught and encouraged in school (Lave 1988). Reports of adults being unable to interpret medical or scientific reports, estimate numbers, and even perform basic calculations such as percentages (Kolata 1997; Hiebert et al. 1997) have led to calls for a quantitative literacy—a general level of comfort with numbers and other quantitative and spatial representations that will enable people to live and work successfully in our increasingly quantitative society. Quantitative literacy involves such actions as being able to set up problems, choose appropriate methods, estimate quantities, and develop a sense of reasonable answers. It is a comfort with numbers, patterns, and space; as Lynne Steen has written, "The new literacy is really about reasoning more than 'rithmetic: assessing claims, detecting fallacies, evaluating risks, weighing evidence" (1997, xix).

It is the task of teachers to prepare students not only for their future courses and study but for engagement in the world. Elliot Eisner puts it simply when he says that "the primary aim of education is not to enable students to do well in school, but to help them do well in the lives they lead outside of school" (2004, 10). This simple fact is often forgotten in the frenzy to prepare students for standardized tests and the demands of future courses. If students are to function effectively as adults in our society, they need to be comfortable with quantitative relationships and they should be prepared to reason mathematically—to question, estimate, and draw conclusions. Through my work with teachers and students in different schools, I have come to appreciate three acts that are critical to the development of quantitative literacy as well as a higher level of mathematical fluency. These three acts—questioning, reasoning, and representing—are often thought of as important aids to learning, but they are all important practices to learn in their own right. They appear in all of the cases we present in this book, but here I will unpack each of the acts and its role in this particular case as a way of exploring and illustrating their importance for students' lives.

Questioning

Most teachers welcome student questions in their classes and regard questions as valuable in the service of learning, yet few teachers explicitly encourage questioning and research shows that student questions are exceptionally rare in schools (Beck 1998), and they become more rare as students move up through school (Good et al. 1987). Additionally, student questioning is generally regarded as a useful process in the pursuit of learning, but questions are rarely considered as a valuable end product in their own right. I would argue that questioning is one of the most important acts that students can learn both for supporting their own learning and becoming literate, well-educated people. As Ciardello (2000) states, "Questioning is both product and process, involving an ongoing interaction between the knower, the known, and sometimes the unknown. It is a branch of knowledge itself" (215). When a student asks a question in a mathematics class, she is actively engaged with the content being studied; she is forming inquiries that will serve to further her understanding and is also thinking about and probing the relationships under consideration. I agree with Ciardello's claim that "to ask a question is an act of cognition and literacy" (2000, 215); indeed, questioning seems to play a critical role in both quantitative and general literacy. When people are given tables of data, or statistical evidence arguing a position, it is essential that they know they can ask questions of the information. "Well-educated people know how to formulate probing questions in the process of educational inquiry" (Ciardello 2000, 215), and they are willing to engage in this cognitive act. F. James Rutherford (1997), representing the American Association for the Advancement of Science, argues that the appropriate response from a quantitatively literate person to a problem such as "A worm traveled 2 meters in 3 hours; what is its speed?" would not be an answer but a series of questions. One appropriate question might be: Was three hours the total elapsed time, or the cumulative time the worm was in motion? I agree that this would be the appropriate response in life, but an entirely different response is generally taught in mathematics classes. Knowing how to ask relevant, probing, and generative questions is critical to functioning successfully in society, yet students are rarely encouraged to ask questions in school mathematics classes and they often fail to engage in this act that is so important to advanced learning and to life.

In addition to the role of questioning in quantitative literacy and more general cognitive engagement, questioning also features centrally in the purest of mathematical work. This is portrayed clearly in the film *A Beautiful Mind*, the biographical account of the mathematician and Nobel Laureate John Nash. The film documents Nash's emotional search for a question that was sufficiently important and interesting to study. The "problem posing" (Silver 1994) he conducted is a central part of the work of academic mathematicians, but questioning on a less grand scale is also critical to most mathematical thinking. Lampert (1990), drawing from Lakatos (1976), depicts mathematical work as a process of zigzagging between conjectures and refutations. When people work on mathematical problems—as mathematicians, engineers, designers, or shoppers—they ask questions of the mathematical situations before them and those questions are central to the knowledge they produce and discover.

As stated earlier, student questioning remains curiously rare in many mathematics classes (Good et al. 1987), with very few teachers focusing upon questioning as a practice to be developed. Cathy, by contrast, encourages student questioning as a deliberate goal. One of the ways that she does this is by asking students to be skeptical and to form probing questions for their peers, whether or not they understand the work. In encouraging skepticism, Cathy uncouples the act of question asking from the stigma of not understanding. She also encourages students to form specific questions in classroom discourse. We saw both types of encouragement in this case as Cathy asked her students to act as skeptics and as she encouraged Stephanie to formulate a *specific* question. After Colin gave his explanation of the algebraic equivalence, Stephanie said "I'm just confused by the whole thing. I don't see how it could work." At this point many teachers would have asked Colin to explain again, or they would have given an explanation themselves. Cathy, however, encouraged the act of student questioning by saying to Stephanie, "Can you frame a question that we could all think about?" Stephanie's question, in turn, prompted Colin to offer a completely different justification for his answer, offering a concrete example that gave other students access to the ideas. This was an important opportunity for Stephanie and others to learn how to pose an important and meaningful question.

Reasoning

The act of mathematical reasoning is central to mathematical work although it is more commonly included in descriptions of literacy. Educated citizens of a quantitative society need to be able to contend, critique, analyze, and deduce—in essence, they need to reason with numbers and mathematical properties. Eisner (2004) highlights the act of reasoning and judgment making, saying that "the disposition and critical acumen that make good judgment possible are among the most important abilities that schools can cultivate in students" (8). The development of reasoning in mathematics classrooms depends upon a particular form of classroom *authority*. If students come to believe that answers are sufficient or correct only when teachers or the book says they are, then they will lack a source of mathematical validation or authority that they can take with them into the world. A more productive source of authority is the domain of mathematics itself, and students who realize they have developed the mathematical tools to *reason* about situations and determine whether they have been correctly answered or interpreted can function well in society. In studies of mathematics classrooms in England and the United States (Boaler 2002b, 2003a), I have observed different versions of authority. In some classrooms the textbook and the teacher are presented as the authority and students always look to them to know if they are moving in the right directions. In other classes teachers tell students that they can determine whether they are correct or moving in the right direction by reasoning mathematically. Teachers can help students learn to reason by asking them to do such things as justify their mathematical claims, explain why something makes sense, and defend their answers and methods to mathematical skeptics.

As students learn to reason, they will also learn what a *reasonable* answer is, which will give them access to the broader number sense that students often lack. Greeno talks about the importance of number sense saying, "People with number sense know where they are in the environment, which things are nearby, which things are easy to reach from where they are, and how routes can be combined flexibly to reach other places efficiently" (1991, 185). The practice of reasoning is a means through which students learn to connect the different places that they visit in the mathematical environment. Students in mathematics classes usually learn environmental landmarks, such as multiplication and division more easily than they learn the important routes between them. For example, many students learn the distributive property in algebra, $a(b + c) = ab + ac$, without realizing that the multiplication algorithm is based upon the same mathematical principles. In Liping Ma's study of the knowledge that a sample of U.S. and Chinese elementary teachers held, she found that Chinese teachers had a good sense of the mathematical environment, thinking about mathematics in terms of "knowledge packages" (1999, 18) and using their network of ideas to help them plan instruction. The U.S. teachers knew important mathematical topics but were not especially cognizant of the links between them. If students learn to reason mathematically, they are more likely to consider and appreciate the fascinating and important network of routes and connections that link mathematical ideas and methods.

Reasoning and sense making are central themes of Cathy's teaching as she consistently asks students to make sense of questions and answers and to justify any claims they make or results they produce. We witnessed students engaging in reasoning both in the small-group interaction between Jose and Antony and in Colin's demonstration at the board. All three of the boys knew that it was insufficient to communicate an answer and that their role must include giving reasons for their ideas. Jose and Antony appeared awkward in their interactions and they may have been inhibited by the presence of the camera, but it is significant that they reasoned their way through their awkwardness, showing their commitment to that process. Cathy's encouragement for students to act as skeptics gives students a further push to reason with clarity and rigor. Cathy engages students in reasoning with a clear purpose: she wants students to make sense of situations and answers in order to *understand* the mathematical ideas.

Representing

The third strand of work that I wish to highlight is that of representing, which, like the acts of questioning and reasoning, is *both* an aid to learning and an important aspect of mathematical literacy. Many of the cases in this book show the students representing their ideas in different ways. In this case we saw ideas represented using algebraic symbols and expressions, numbers, and pictures. In other cases we saw students representing their ideas using number lines, pie charts, three-dimensional cylinders, and so on. Representations are a critical form of literacy. Eisner proposes that "meaning systems" conveyed through varied representations give access to life itself (1998, 12) and that "different forms of representation evoke, develop, and refine the modes of thinking that contribute to the cultivation of what is broadly called *mind*" (2004, 9). The role of representation in mathematical work is well recognized, as proficient mathematicians frequently use representations in order to solve problems and communicate results (Schoenfeld 1985). Adults in mathematical jobs such as engineering and construction frequently represent their ideas as part of their work (Gainsburg 2003), both for understanding and communicating. Eisner (1998) claims that representation has four important roles—the opportunity to stabilize ideas; the opportunity to edit, refine, and produce clarity and elegance; the opportunity to communicate with others; and the opportunity to discover—as representation does not just entail the performance of an idea but can also engender the creation of an idea. The opportunities that representations afford are minimized if students are given repeated experience with only one type of representation, such as numbers. Varied representations of mathematical ideas are immensely valuable in classrooms—they give different access to the ideas being discussed; they encourage students to transform ideas into multiple forms, thus deepening understanding; they encourage learning of an important form of literacy; and they teach students an essential communicative and problem-solving tool.

In this particular case we saw the idea of algebraic equivalence communicated in three very different ways that came about through different representations. Colin communicated his first explanation of the equivalence of the expression through algebraic symbols. As he reasoned through the equivalence, it was clear that some students followed and understood. Later, in response to Stephanie's question, he represented the ideas using a particular numeric example, which gave other students access to the ideas. Later in the lesson Cathy asked Melissa to show her diagrammatic representation of the ideas. Melissa also drew from a particular numeric case, representing the numbers as rectangles, but it was apparent that this different representation gave even more students access to the idea of equivalence. Melissa's presentation was not especially polished and she struggled to communicate her idea clearly, but struggle is part of classroom life, and in some ways it made her contribution more important to include for consideration. The example showed a student who was skirting on the edge between using ideas to show something and using ideas to prove something; this is an interesting and important place for students to be.

—

I have highlighted the three acts of questioning, reasoning, and representing, partly because they can be seen in all of the teaching cases in this book and they are valued and deliberate outcomes of Cathy's pedagogical decisions and also because I regard the three acts as critical in the formation of quantitative literacy. Many teachers would like their students to ask probing questions, reason mathematically, and represent ideas in different ways but do not find students willing to do so. The students in these cases engage so fluently in these three important practices because of the pedagogical decisions that Cathy has made and the "interactional routines" (Lampert 1990) that she has carefully established in the classroom. Cathy's encouragement of questioning, reasoning, and representing helps students learn a form of mathematical literacy that will serve them well in our quantitative society and give them access to higher-level mathematical work.

Chapter 7

Class Participation
Through the Eyes of Students (May 23)

Mathematics classrooms are more likely to be places in which mathematical proficiency develops when they are communities of learners and not collections of isolated individuals.

KILPATRICK, SWAFFORD, AND FINDELL (2001, 425)

If you want students to understand, then be sure they are reflecting on what they are doing and communicating it to others.

HIEBERT ET AL. (1997, 18)

Background of the Lesson—Cathy's Perspective

I want students to understand. I want them to communicate their thinking coherently and clearly. I want my classroom to be a community of learners. But learning to effectively manage classroom discourse is an ongoing process. I vividly recall the day more than fifteen years ago when, inspired by a weekend workshop on cooperative learning, I returned to my classroom and moved the desks into groups of four. Not surprisingly, the arrangement of the furniture did not result in significant changes in the students' dialogue, or in what or how much they learned. Since then, I have spent a lot of time thinking, talking with colleagues, and experimenting with strategies to create a classroom culture in which students exchange ideas, both in small groups and in the forum of whole-class discussions, as a community that truly supports the learning of all students.

Managing whole-class discussions, though, is challenging. The following excerpt from *Adding It Up: Helping Children Learn Mathematics* reveals some of the complexity involved:

78

Teachers must make judgments about when to tell, when to question, and when to correct. They must decide when to guide with prompting and when to let the students grapple with a mathematical issue. They also need to decide who should get the floor in whole-group discussions and how turns should be allocated. Teachers have the responsibility for moving the mathematics along while affording students opportunities to offer solutions, make claims, answer questions, and provide explanations to their colleagues. (Kilpatrick, Swafford, and Findell 2001, 345)

This in itself requires knowledge and skill. But besides knowing the terrain of the mathematics well enough to help students build mathematically significant ideas, teachers must also address the affective issues of discourse. Helping students learn why talking about mathematics is important to their learning, helping them to learn to talk in constructive, respectful ways, helping them learn to listen and to value and build on the thinking of their peers—all of these elements are essential for conducting a mathematically productive discussion.

This makes teachers somewhat dependent on their students for the success of a discussion (Chazan 2000, 120). There are always students who thrive on sharing their ideas and theories with the class, others who don't mind doing so if they are prodded a little, and those who, for whatever reason, simply never volunteer. Depending upon the proportions of those three groups, classes can have lively interchanges, unproductive silences, or something in between. NCTM's *Professional Standards for Teaching Mathematics* discusses what teachers need to consider as they orchestrate a discourse that will give all students access to the important mathematics:

Who is volunteering comments and who is not? How are students responding to one another? . . . Teachers must be committed to engaging *every* student in contributing to the thinking of the class. . . . They must make sensitive decisions about how turns to speak are shared in the large group—for example, whom to call on when and whether to call on particular students who do not volunteer. (NCTM 1991, 36; italics mine)

Herein lies the dilemma that is the focus of this case. For years I have believed there is no need for every student to contribute to whole-class discussions as long as all students contribute their ideas in small collaborative groups. I know that analytical thinking is more difficult during emotional stress, and I know that middle school students are at a fragile age where they are particularly sensitive to the opinions of their classmates. I have also become aware that many students, whose reasoning and confidence have been eroded over the years, do not think they have much to contribute to a mathematical discussion. Mathematical ideas have not made sense to many of them for so long that they don't feel like their ideas are of substance, and being expected to share them can be very painful. My thinking has been that if students are anxious about being called on, then their learning will be hindered. So I have told many classes, "I will never put you on the spot," and have relied instead on hand raising.

Hand raising, however, has its costs. In some classes a few students—and rarely any others—volunteer for every question. And while a silent student may well be engaged in learning by listening closely, it is possible that students who never volunteer—and know they will never be required to speak to the class— may not feel accountable to listen to or analyze the ideas being considered. This may also mean that they think they are not accountable to learn. The idea that *every* student's voice needs to be heard by the entire class is stressed in *Making Sense* (Hiebert et al. 1997): "To the extent that some students are excluded and do not participate, the learning possibilities are diminished for everyone" (67). This statement, with its focus on equity, gave me a new way to think about participation. Saying, "You must be accountable to listening and thinking," is very different from saying, "We need your voice; we need to hear how you are thinking; otherwise, none of us will learn as much." I thought that middle school students would respond positively to this difference in intention.

My reading and thinking prompted me to talk to the students about why it was important that all students contribute to a discussion. I then began employing a strategy that I thought would increase the potential for everyone's voice to be heard while minimizing anxiety. Prior to a whole-class discussion, students would discuss the problem or question in small groups; then I would randomly call on someone to report for his or her group. This, it seemed, would make it safe to call on anyone because if students were reporting what the group had talked about, the group would share responsibility for the answer. This way everyone's voice, over time, would have the potential of being heard. While this was not the only strategy I used for discussions, I did use it regularly. In the clip that accompanies this chapter, the issue came to a head—and I was in for a surprise.

Prior to the Video Selection

The class had been working on finding the surface area of rectangular prisms. We began class that day by correcting homework in groups; then I gave them the dimensions of an arbitrary rectangular prism—3 by 4 by 5—and asked the groups to discuss what the dimensions of each of its faces would be. I decided to randomly appoint a spokesperson for each group and then randomly choose a group to begin the whole-class discussion. I told the class that each spokesperson would need to be ready to explain what the dimensions of each of the faces would be as well as how his or her group had figured it out. I would roll a die (whose numbers corresponded to the table numbers) to determine which group would report first. The video selection begins as I roll the die.

◉Watch "Class Participation: Through the Eyes of Students," CD 2

Lesson Analysis and Reflection

When Randy froze, I was transported back years earlier to a ski resort, where I had been perched high on the edge of a bowl. The other people in my class had already traversed across its face, but I was unable to move. This may have been how Randy felt; he seemed utterly unable to speak. I felt bad to have put him in this position, knowing that this was exactly what I had been trying to avoid.

My thinking about class discussions was based on articles, research, and discussions with colleagues, but I had not asked the students! I have often found that asking students' opinions about issues that arise in class—mathematical or not—can help build the sense of community so necessary to the productive exchange of mathematical ideas. Magdalene Lampert describes this as building "academic character" and says that

> the work of maintaining productive relationships with and among students must include simultaneous attention both to academic identity and to progress. The fragility of individual identity in the school context is a problem for the teacher because it can get in the way of improving academic performance. In this domain, particularly, doing the work of teaching requires the cooperation of one's students. If a student is unable to feel that it is safe to have and express ideas, or even to answer a simple question, then performance will not be improved. The goal of actions described by these terms is not consistency per se or even a trusting relationship, but a set of relationships that make it likely that students will engage in activities that will lead to learning. (2001, 266)

Randy's silence presented a problem, and rather than move on, I knew it was time—perhaps long overdue—to hear from my students.

I started by talking about a friend's experience in high school, an experience that had made a big impression on me at the time. I wanted to acknowledge that talking in front of our peers is not easy for everyone. Middle school students are at an age where they are acutely aware of what others think of them, and their teachers often forget how high the stakes can be when we ask them to lay bare

81

their thinking. The class was very quiet at first, so I kept talking to help them realize how sincerely I wanted to hear what they had to say.

I was surprised, then, when Artie, who had seemed to be an eager participant all year, raised his hand to respond, saying, "You might not understand what everyone is talking about." I realized he was talking about the difficulty of reporting *for a group*. Alicia and Christine readily followed up with different perspectives on what made that so difficult. Alicia talked about being the reporter and "not knowing what you're talking about—at all—and not having enough time to figure out what we're talking about." Christine said that she would rather report "just for me, but not for my group" because she was afraid she would get it wrong and her group would be upset with her.

I decided then that it was important to explain why I thought it was critical for all students to talk to the class. I wanted them to understand that I had reasons, which were important to me, for asking them to do this—and I wanted to know what I could do to make it easier for them to speak. Gradually the students started opening up. As they spoke, I was surprised at the level of anxiety they had about having to report for their groups. I had been so sure that, in employing this technique, I was *reducing* the pressure on students, but except for Brittani, the overwhelming opinion seemed to be that the pressure was much greater. As Zach said, "You might get somebody else's opinion wrong." The fear of misrepresenting what their group discussed, as well as the difficulty of summarizing multiple points of view, was much more stressful for them than being asked to give their own ideas. After hearing their ideas, this made sense, but if I hadn't allowed this opportunity for discussion, I never would have known how they felt.

It was when I mentioned Popsicle® sticks that the discussion really heated up. I knew that this strategy, intended to promote accountability, equity, and fairness in "air time" (Gilbert 2001, 18) had been used in their sixth-grade mathematics class. In this approach for selecting students to speak, each student's name is written on a tongue depressor or ice cream stick. Then, when the teacher poses a question, he or she randomly selects a stick and the child whose name is on the stick is supposed to answer the question. I had never used this strategy with students for a variety of reasons, and I was curious what they thought about it. Kara talked about an experience when she was "totally and completely embarrassed in front of the whole class." Sarah talked about how she had wanted to answer questions but never got called on. Alicia said she was "cool with Popsicle® sticks" as long as there was no anger or criticism if she didn't know the answer. I was amazed to see how passionate they were.

As I tried to find my way through this discussion, I again told the students why I think talking about math is so important. But the discussion about being embarrassed rapidly turned to the issue of being right. Again, I was surprised—and disappointed. From the first day of class, I had, at every opportunity, tried to impress upon my students the importance and necessity of mistakes. I wanted my students to believe that, as Hiebert et al. say, "mistakes must be seen by the students and the teacher as places that afford opportunities to examine errors in reasoning and thereby raise everyone's level of analysis" (1997, 9). I had also tried to help them realize how important confusion is and that "partially grasped ideas and periods of confusion are a natural part of the process of developing understanding" (California State Department of Education 1987, 14). I continually emphasized that wrong answers and confusion are valuable, *if* students reflect on and confront the ideas, and that real learning requires some struggle, some confusion, and a lot of figuring out. Despite this yearlong effort to change students' orientation from worshipping the quick, right answer to valuing the act of figuring things out (Duckworth 1987), I heard loud and clear on this day that, for at least the students who spoke, being wrong was still equated with not being smart. And everyone wants to feel smart! It was clear that changing students' beliefs about learning takes a very long time.

As the class left, I was brimming with questions and wonderings. How important is it, really, for *every* student's voice to be heard in whole-class discussions? How important are whole-class discussions? Some colleagues I greatly respect rarely conduct these discussions, opting instead for small-group discussions. How can we help students really believe that being smart—and mathematically proficient—means being able to play with mathematical ideas, take wrong courses, and learn from our wrong turns? Even in this class, where the students had fairly strong mathematical egos, after almost a whole year of being told that mistakes are valuable, the risk of being wrong or misrepresenting one's peers was still intimidating.

We were very close to the end of the year; there were only thirteen more days of instruction. I stopped, temporarily at least, using the strategy of having students report for their groups and returned to relying on volunteers. It was interesting, though, that after this conversation, there was a different feeling in the class. I started to hear a lot from students who had been virtually silent all year, and I noticed a camaraderie that made conversations flow more easily. I noticed something else too: this discussion left me feeling closer to my students. I appreciated their honesty in a relationship that is a true partnership, and I knew it was time well spent in our path toward building both academic character and academic achievement.

Case Commentary—Jo's Analysis

Why Mathematical Discussions?

Mathematical discussions are extremely important, for a number of reasons. When students discuss a mathematical idea, they come to know that mathematics is more than a collection of rules and methods set out in books; they realize that mathematics is a subject that they can have ideas about, a subject that can invoke different perspectives and methods and one that is connected through organizing concepts and themes. In addition, it is critically important for children, especially developing adolescents, to know that they can offer their own ideas and perspectives when working on mathematics; when they do not, they often feel disempowered and disenfranchised, ultimately choosing to leave mathematics even when they have performed well (Boaler and Greeno 2000). When students are asked to give their ideas on mathematical problems, they feel that they are engaging in an intellectual act and that they have agency. Mathematical discussions also give access points to many different students, serving as a highly important pedagogical resource to teachers who have students with vastly different understandings and backgrounds. When students are asked to justify and give reasons, and to explain in different ways, some students develop deeper understanding through the act of explaining, while others are given additional access into the ideas (Boaler 2003a). Perhaps most importantly, mathematical discussions are important because students who are talking about mathematics are also engaged. Schwartz (1999) has talked about the act of connecting to another person's ideas, pointing out that collaboration occurs when one person forms a model or representation of another person's thoughts. This is a highly sophisticated intellectual act that involves listening carefully and making an effort to produce shared mathematical meaning (Sherin, Louis, and Mendez 2000). Students enjoy having mathematical discussions, they report that they learn a great deal from them (Boaler 2000), and they are engaged in an act of mathematical reflection and representation that aids learning in unparalleled ways.

Why Whole-Class Discussions?

Not all mathematical discussions are productive and teachers have to choose topics for discussion carefully; they also need to establish careful social norms that induce respect, and sociomathematical norms (Yackel and Cobb 1996) that encourage justification and reasoning. During whole-class discussions, teachers must simultaneously attend to the needs of individuals and those of the whole class (Lampert 2001). Some highly effective teachers rarely ask classes to engage in whole-class discussions, relying instead upon small-group discussions. The balance between small- and whole-class discussion is something that individual teachers must decide on in response to the needs of their classes, but whole-class discussions afford some specific opportunities that teachers may want to draw upon at times. In particular, they allow teachers to model and encourage mathematical behavior that they hope students will emulate in small groups. Lampert (1990) gives an account of her own teaching and talks about the role of whole-class discussion in modeling certain behaviors:

To communicate the idea that I thought every answer was (or should be) arrived at by a process of reasoning that makes sense to the person who volunteered it, I asked the class, "Can anyone explain what they thought so-and-so was thinking?" and "Why would it make sense to think that?" And then I asked the person who gave the answer to respond. This routine was a way of modeling talk about thinking. It also made thinking into a public and collaborative activity, wherein students would rehearse the sort of intellectual courage, intellectual honesty, and wise restraint that Polya considered essential to doing mathematics. (40–41)

Methods of Encouraging Student Participation

In the class period that is the focus of this case, the students did not have a mathematical discussion, but a discussion about student participation. This was an important event because it helped Cathy learn about the most appropriate ways to encourage students to participate. Cathy, like Lampert, places great value upon whole-class discussions and she engages in many different practices to encourage students to talk. In this case we saw Cathy asking a student to report for his group, with the idea that it would be less threatening for the student to report a conversation from the group than to give his own thoughts or ideas. But events did not unfold as Cathy expected and the subsequent discussion gave us important insights into students' feelings and perspectives. In this class period, in which we heard from almost all the students in the class about their feelings on the act of discussion, the students told Cathy that reporting for the group put them under *more* pressure. Some students were more nervous about misrepresenting their group than they were about getting an answer wrong. But what does this mean for the particular strategy Cathy employs? There is value in hearing from different groups, and the limitations of always asking for volunteers are obvious. In this case Cathy assigned reporters, so students knew they were going to be reporting for their group, but the first assigned reporter appeared paralyzed when it was time to talk about his group's ideas. Sarah offered an interesting thought in the subsequent discussion; she suggested that it would be preferable if students were asked to report on the *ideas they got* from the group, rather than the group discussion itself. Another strategy would involve the group members deciding what the reporter would talk about before the group time ended. None of the strategies is perfect; they each have strengths and weaknesses that will depend upon the situation in which they are used, revealing again the complex and "situational" (Bolster 1983, 296) nature of teaching. Lampert's (1985) description of teaching as an act of "dilemma management" involving the resolution of practical dilemmas and conceptual paradoxes is apt.

Equitable Participation of Students

Cathy's class did not engage in whole-class discussions all of the time, although this impression may be gained from our overrepresentation of this particular practice in the video cases. The students also engaged in many different pedagogical practices that we do not show in the videos; for example, they worked individually and in small groups, using a range of resources such as worksheets, traditional texts, and longer problems. The predominance of class discussion in the cases comes about partly because the students' conversations give clear access to the collective work of the class. The preponderance of this particular practice also means that viewers can consider the practice in some depth. I have watched several of the cases from this book with other teachers. Inevitably one of the questions that is raised by teachers concerns the number of students who spoke. Teachers will often watch five or ten minutes of a discussion and comment that "only six students spoke" or "only ten students spoke." This is a concern, shared by most teachers, about the equitable involvement of all students. Such a concern is important, but it seems somewhat misplaced when viewing a case of teaching for a number of reasons. First, it seems that people make such comments only when some students are contributing to ideas; if no students contribute, and only the teacher talks, they do not worry. This raises an inevitable question: Why is a discussion involving ten students worse than one involving none? The students in Cathy's classes reported in interviews (see CD 2) that they were more interested when they heard different people contribute to ideas than when they heard only from the teacher. They communicated that different student ideas were valuable, even when they themselves were not talking. Concerns about the number of students speaking also seem misplaced as we generally see a small fraction of class time when we view cases; it is tempting to count the number of students, or proportions of girls or boys, who speak, but another twenty seconds of the lesson might give a completely different impression of participation. More substantively, it seems inappropriate to equate students who speak with students who are engaged. Whenever Cathy starts a class discussion, she hopes that as many students as possible will contribute. She holds this goal because she knows that students who discuss ideas are also engaged in thinking about them. But this does not mean that students who are quiet are not engaged; some students do not want to take part in a discussion but learn a great deal from the ideas that are collectively developed. We can probably all remember discussions in which we were personally engaged even when not speaking.

Focusing upon the Mathematical Flow

Teachers' concerns for the equal participation of students give us insights into an important dilemma that teachers face when they conduct class discussions—that of hearing from as many students as possible while at the same time developing the most productive mathematical flow of ideas. This is a dilemma Deborah Ball reflects upon when she talks of her desire to "teach students with intellectual honesty, to value their interests and also connect them to ideas and traditions growing out of centuries of mathematics exploration and invention" (1993, 375). A teacher's role includes valuing and encouraging student ideas while also guiding students toward important mathematical goals. Teaching through class discussions is not easy; it requires a range of pedagogical practices and it stretches even the most accomplished and experienced teachers as they respond to a range of student responses in the moment. Sherin (2002) studied accomplished teachers conducting whole-class discussions and identified the "tensions" they faced, such as moving between what she calls *process* and *content*. "Process refers to how the teachers and students interact in discussions, who talks to whom, when and in what ways. . . . The content of the discourse, in contrast, refers to the mathematical substance of the ideas raised, to the depth and complexity of these ideas in terms of the mathematical concepts under discussion" (209). Sherin draws attention to the balance teachers need to maintain between teaching students *how* to engage in class and focusing upon content.

Another important tension teachers face concerns *who* talks in class, as teachers need to both involve and honor different students' ideas, as well as enable a coherent and relatively efficient mathematical discussion. I think of this dilemma in terms of a continuum (see Figure 7–1).

At one end of the continuum is the teacher who seeks to involve all students at all times; teachers who have this as their primary goal would be likely to ask all students or all groups of students to report their thinking in a discussion. The other end of the continuum represents a mathematical progression of ideas that is controlled by the teacher and relatively efficient. A teacher located at this end of the continuum would probably do all of the talking herself. A little distance from the right end of the continuum would be teachers who ask only some students to report out, those they know have correct answers or who will move the thinking of the class forward. There is no correct place for a teacher to locate herself—in some situations it is best for the teacher or a small number of students to talk; in others it may be appropriate to hear from all students. But my studies of successful teachers in the United States, along with Staples' study of a teacher who brought about highly productive discussions (Staples 2004), suggest that teachers

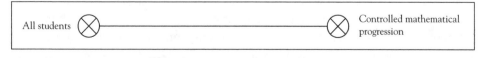

All students ⊗————————————————⊗ Controlled mathematical progression

Figure 7–1.

need to pay careful attention to this issue and that it is critical to consider the shape, flow, and direction of the mathematical ideas that are produced in discussion, as well as the involvement of students. Our studies have revealed that the more successful teachers strive to involve as many students as possible, but they also enact a number of practices that maintain respect for the "integrity of mathematics" (Ball 1993, 373). These include

- strategically calling on particular students at times, knowing they will ask a good question or offer a helpful representation of ideas
- asking a student to hold on to a thought if it threatens to take the direction in one the teacher feels would not be productive
- asking a student who has produced interesting work to prepare something to show others
- stressing the importance of particular students' comments, using tone and emphasis to highlight certain ideas
- adding ideas, questions, and linkages between different student ideas

Ball describes her dual focus on students and mathematics eloquently: "With my ears to the ground, listening to my students, my eyes are focused on the mathematical horizon" (1993, 376).

The act of teaching through class discussions is complex, and teachers need to employ a range of pedagogical moves while maintaining attention to content, process, and students. The issue that is reflected in this case, of whom to call on in class and how, is just one of the dilemmas teachers face as they conduct class discussions (Sherin 2002; Sherin, Louis, and Mendez 2000; Hufferd-Ackles, Fuson, and Sherin 2004). We hope that the students who shared their ideas in this case will be a helpful resource for teachers as they choose between the different methods for encouraging student participation.

The Renewed Participation of Alicia and Brittani

One of Cathy's goals for the year was to involve as many students as possible in discussion. Alicia and Brittani were not confident students and they were fairly reticent in class discussions. Brittani was especially quiet and had not offered her ideas before the discussion in this case. From this lesson on, both girls' participation changed and readers will see their active involvement in subsequent cases. The event that seemed to have prompted this additional engagement was the discussion in this case. Cathy was surprised (and pleased) to hear from Brittani and Alicia in that discussion. I have watched this case a number of times with groups of teachers, and observers often comment that only some students are talking and they are probably the ones who feel comfortable doing so. There is often surprise when I tell them that Brittani and Alicia, both contributors to the discussion, had rarely spoken before. It is highly significant that this discussion appeared to transform the subsequent engagement of the two girls.

A number of studies have shown that students rate the presence of *caring adults* (Davidson and Phelan 1999) as the most significant factor in their involvement with school. During the discussion, Cathy told students that getting them to talk and feel involved was "really important" to her; she talked openly, communicating her concern for their involvement and her respect for their ideas. It is not hard to imagine that this class discussion encouraged the girls to feel part of a common endeavor and to feel that their ideas and involvement in discussion really were important to the teacher. Fredricks, Blumenfeld, and Paris (2004) report that students cite one of the most important factors in being motivated at school is feeling part of a collective, a group working together rather than individuals in competition with others. In interviews at the end of the year, Alicia chose to talk about the class discussion in which they shared their feelings, saying that it was a "really good" discussion and that it had caused more students to participate. She also reported that it was the first time the teacher had "acknowledged that sometimes it hurts to be proved wrong in front of the class." This was interesting to me; prior to that point Cathy had stressed on many occasions that it was good to share wrong answers, as they could be sites for learning, but it mattered to Alicia that Cathy acknowledged that it could also be painful. The conversation seemed to convey to Alicia (and probably others) that Cathy cared about them and was respectful of their feelings. In the same interview, Sarah said, "Ms. Humphreys respects us and there's not a lot of teachers that respect the students." Wentzel (1997) asked adolescent students about the kinds of behavior they interpreted as caring. In their responses, "students described teachers who tried to make classes interesting; who talked and listened to them; who were honest, fair, and trusting; and who showed concern for them as individuals by asking whether they needed help, making sure they understood what was being taught, and asking them if something was wrong" (Fredricks, Blumenfeld, and Paris 2004). Cathy communicated many of these qualities in the class discussion and it seemed that Alicia and Brittani responded very positively to them.

Psychological research on motivation and engagement in school has produced clear evidence about the factors that are important to students; these include feeling part of a collective identity, or commonality; caring adults; connectedness with the values and goals of schooling; and opportunity to demonstrate competence and to work on cognitively demanding work (Fredricks, Blumerfeld, and Paris 2004). When psychological research on motivation and engagement is brought to bear on this case, and the renewed engagement of Alicia and Brittani in particular, we may learn something about the importance of the discussion Cathy held with her students. Sarah, in her interview, astutely pointed out that "it would have been good if it had happened earlier," which certainly seems to be the case when we see the renewed participation of the two girls. But such discussions are extremely unusual in mathematics classes. When teachers do talk openly about their goals and wishes for students, it is often at the start of the year. Part of the effectiveness of the discussion derived from its timing and the responsiveness of Cathy to the events that prompted the discussion. As a researcher I have had the luxury of holding many conversations with students of middle and high school age about their mathematics teaching and learning environments and the aspects they find particularly helpful or unhelpful. In all of those conversations I have found students to be extremely perceptive and insightful about ways to improve teaching; they also speak with great consideration for other students, choosing to give careful ideas that would benefit everyone. Yet there are few or no venues in school for students' ideas about teaching to be heard. A worthwhile goal for teachers who would like to receive such input might be to create such venues for their own students, whether they be written reflections, small-group or individual interviews, or even whole-class discussions, as we saw in this case.

Chapter 8

Volume of Prisms and Cylinders
Extending Prior Knowledge
(June 5)

*With my ears to the ground, listening to my students, my eyes are
focused on the mathematical horizon.*

BALL (1993, 376)

*Adaptive reasoning refers to the capacity to think logically about the
relationships among concepts and situations. . . . In mathematics,
adaptive reasoning is the glue that holds everything together, the
lodestar that guides learning.*

KILPATRICK, SWAFFORD, AND FINDELL (2001, 129)

Background of the Lesson—Cathy's Perspective

Middle school students usually experience surface area and volume by learning
and applying formulas. Most textbooks approach these measurement ideas by
showing pictures of two- or three-dimensional figures, introducing a formula with
diagrams to show why the formula works, and following up with examples and
exercises. And while accurate and efficient use of formulas is an essential tool in
mathematics, students who have not had an opportunity to think deeply about
what these concepts mean, or to experience the mathematical relationships
involved, often apply formulas blindly and inappropriately. As an example, I share
this personal vignette:

John was my student in an advanced seventh-grade class. I had given students
the task of building complicated three-dimensional figures with linking cubes and
then finding their volumes and surface areas. After John built one such figure, he

came up to me, holding it in his hands. "Mrs. Humphreys," he said, "you can't find the volume of this, because volume is length times width times height."

I wasn't sure what to make of this. Since John could easily have counted the cubes, I wondered if he understood the concept of volume at all. He seemed to think that the formula he had learned *was* volume. One thing was certain: John had not built an understanding of volume that would enable him to know when to apply that particular formula or when a different formula or approach was called for. And while this example made a long-lasting impression on me, the kind of thinking John demonstrated is not unusual. Many of my students over the years have displayed an "instrumental" understanding (Skemp 1978) of measurement ideas—an understanding that relies on the possession and use of tools (in this case, formulas)—rather than a "relational" understanding, which would allow them to know their way around the landscape of two- and three-dimensional measurement and understand which tools were effective for which tasks, and why.

Another recent publication has given me a different lens through which to view John's difficulty. In *Adding It Up: Helping Children Learn Mathematics* (Kilpatrick, Swafford, and Findell 2001), mathematical proficiency is envisioned as a thick rope composed of five "interwoven and interdependent" strands (5): procedural fluency, productive disposition, conceptual understanding, adaptive reasoning, and strategic competence. None of these strands alone is strong enough for a child to be successful in learning mathematics. For John, as for so many students I've known, the procedural fluency that he relied upon was not enough to support him in a new situation.

In order to help students acquire mathematical proficiency with volume and surface area, I was lucky to be able to use the unit *Filling and Wrapping* (Lappan et al. 1998a), from the *Connected Mathematics Project*, which builds conceptual understanding, strategic thinking, and adaptive reasoning together with the procedural fluency that dominates most textbooks. In this unit, students gain proficiency with surface area and volume by first building conceptual understanding through solving problems and by making use of what they have learned about two-dimensional shapes. Our class had just finished the first three investigations of this unit. In one of these, the students had made flat patterns (nets) for right rectangular prisms and had used those nets to determine the surface areas of the prisms. Many students had struggled with moving fluidly between a three-dimensional prism and its two-dimensional flat pattern. It surprised me that the relationships between the dimensions of a box and the dimensions of the rectangular sectors on its flat pattern were not apparent, and it was fun watching students gradually make those connections. In another investigation, the students had encountered conservation of volume by building prisms with the same volume but different dimensions; they had investigated the change in surface area as the dimensions changed. Until this day's lesson, however, our class had not yet calculated volumes using a formula, although I was aware that some students may have done so in earlier grades.

Because we were in the last week of instruction for the school year, I knew I would not be able to finish the unit, which involves volumes and surface areas of nonrectangular right prisms, cylinders, cones, and spheres. Since we would not have time to derive formulas for each of these figures, I decided that it was important for the students to think about volume in general. I knew that many students had heard and used the formula $V = l \times w \times h$ but wondered if any of them had thought about why it makes sense. I thought that if students could understand the sense in this particular formula, then they would more easily understand the general notion that the volume of any prism or cylinder is equal to the area of its base times the height. So I planned to devote one class period to making sense of this formula and a second class period to generalizing about volume.

The day prior to the lesson on this video selection, I gave the students pictures of three rectangular prisms and asked them to figure out mentally how many cubes would be required to build each. Then I had them explain to their group not only what they got, but how they had figured it out. As I listened to these discussions, I learned that most of the students had multiplied the dimensions. When I opened the discussion to the whole class, Kara said that she had multiplied "length times width times height." I asked the students how many of them had learned this formula before they came to seventh grade and more than half of them raised their hands. I then gave them two questions to consider in their small groups:

1. Why does length times width times height ($l \times w \times h$) make sense as a make sense as a way of finding the volume of a rectangular prism?
2. When would $l \times w \times h$ NOT work for volume?

They spent about ten minutes talking about this; as I walked around listening, I heard several students talking about "layers." Alicia then called me aside and said she couldn't figure it out; she said that she always knew it was $l \times w \times h$ but "they didn't tell us why!" Sometimes formulas are presented without explanation, but most teachers want to make sure that students understand the reasoning behind formulas and do present explanations for why they work. But there is a world of difference between telling students why something makes sense and giving them them the opportunity to make sense of it for themselves. Talking and writing about their ideas allow students to clarify what they truly understand and to also see the limits of their understanding.

We were close to the end of the period, so I asked students when they thought $l \times w \times h$ would not work. Most of the groups said that it wouldn't work with two-dimensional shapes. Michael said that they also thought it wouldn't work with something like a sphere. I told the students to think about these ideas that evening and I assured them that we would continue with this discussion the next day.

Prior to the Video Selection

The next day, while the students were correcting their homework, I put a rectangular prism built of linking cubes on each table. Then I called the class to attention and asked for volunteers to make a convincing argument for why the volume of a rectangular prism could be found by multiplying the length and width and height. Many students volunteered to do so, always using their prisms to help them. Ben, Ariel, Sarah, Alicia, and Christine were the first to share; Michael, Artie, and Evan followed. Although all of their ideas included the notion of figuring out the number of cubes in the bottom layer and then multiplying that by the number of layers, each person had a somewhat different way of putting this into words. Then, in order to assess every student's thinking, I gave each person a 3-by-5-inch card and asked them to use words and pictures to explain why the formula made sense. (See Figures 8–1 through 8–3.) As they were writing, I thought about how to pose the next problem.

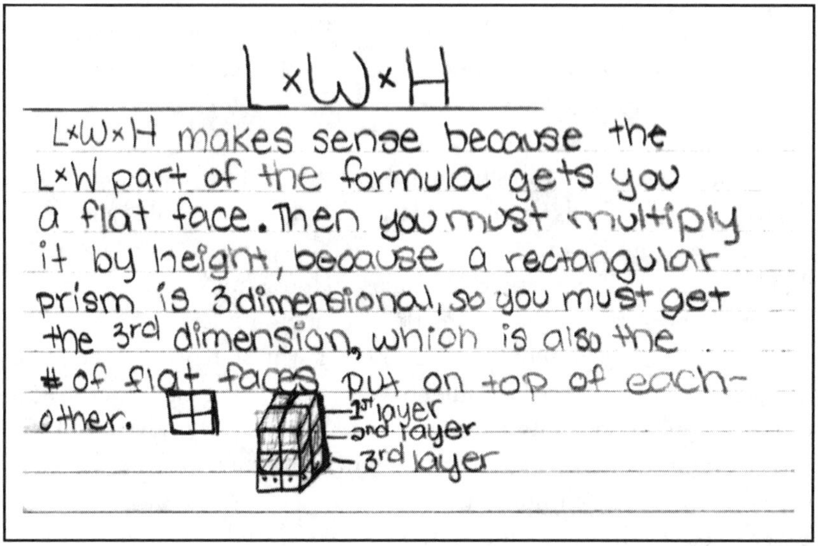
L×W×H

L×W×H makes sense because the L×W part of the formula gets you a flat face. Then you must multiply it by height, because a rectangular prism is 3dimensional, so you must get the 3rd dimension, which is also the # of flat faces put on top of each-other.

Figure 8–1.

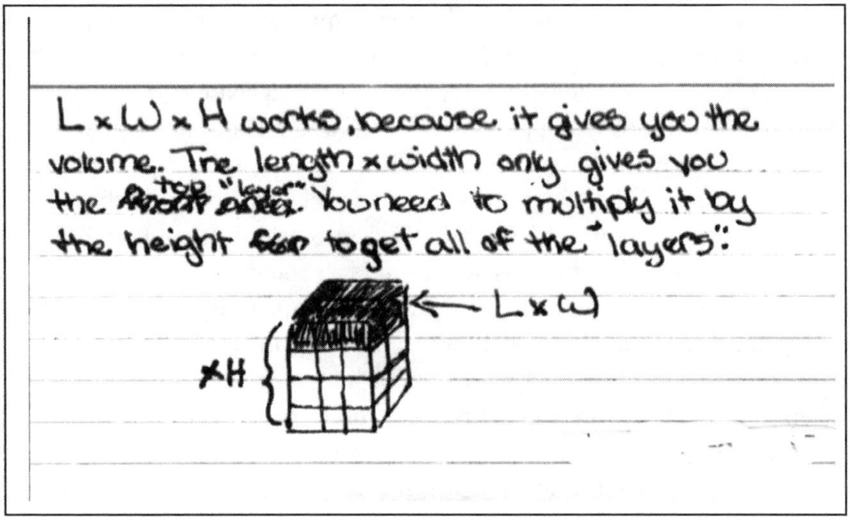

L x W x H works, because it gives you the volume. The length x width only gives you the ~~front~~ top "layer". You need to multiply it by the height ~~ffo~~ to get all of the "layers".

Figure 8–2.

Length x Width x Height works because the length x width is finding the amount of cubes in a layer and the height figures how many layers

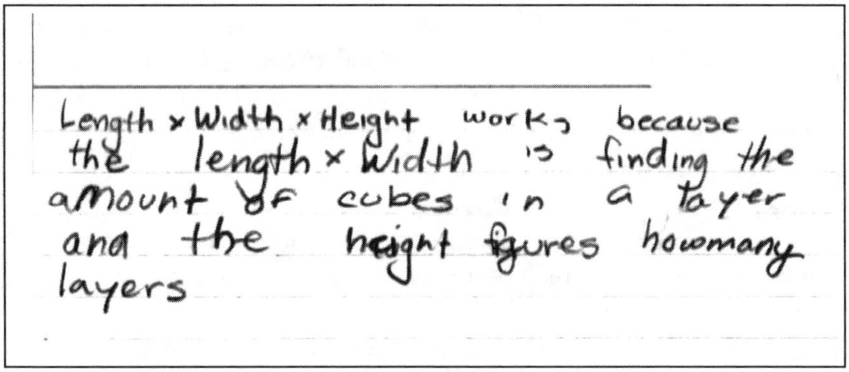

Figure 8–3.

Watch "Volume of Prisms and Cylinders: Extending Prior Knowledge," CD 2

Lesson Analysis and Reflection

The question about whether there were more cylinders or more rectangular prisms in a grocery store occurred to me as I was holding up the dried oats container. We all got caught up in wondering about it, and I know that we could have had a valuable statistical investigation about this if school weren't about to end! But this wasn't an option, so I regained the students' attention. Since my goal was to have students think about volume in general, I was careful to make my question a general one. "Is there anything about rectangular prisms that could help us have a theory about how to find the volume of one of these [a cylinder]?"

Amy, who relied on strong procedural skills and a good memory, was first to venture an idea. When I heard her say, "The area . . . of the cylinder?" I wasn't sure what she meant. Time in the classroom is precious, and a teacher is always balancing the ideas of content with the different tensions of valuing individuals' ideas and the needs of the students as a group. It is something of a tightrope walk requiring constant decision making. Since Amy hadn't referred to rectangular prisms at all, I made a quick decision not to press her further but rather to gather more ideas for consideration before deciding which of the ideas to focus on.

Then Yvette, who was normally reticent, used the oats container to demonstrate her theory that its volume could be obtained by finding the area of the circular base and multiplying that by its height. Michael built on what Yvette had said by contributing the idea of layers and making a direct connection to the earlier class discussion about the layers in rectangular prisms. Since this was exactly the connection I was hoping for, I could have stopped the conversation rather than entertaining more ideas. I have learned, however, that just because an important relationship has been publicly stated, whether by a student or by the teacher, it cannot be assumed that everyone else has understood it. The relationships that Michael and Yvette had raised were ideas that each student would need to construct for himself or herself. Explanations, no matter how clear, cannot provide understanding of relationships; that important work must be done by each individual (Kamii and Warrington 1999). So I needed to persist in pressing to see how others were thinking about the ideas that Yvette and Michael had raised, which could give each student more opportunity to build the foundation for a powerful understanding of volume.

Alicia immediately showed me why my decision to continue the discussion was so important. She first used Yvette's idea by explaining how she could find the area of the base of a cylinder, but she couldn't tell yet why Yvette's idea made sense. All she could say was that it "seemed like the right thing to do." Yet she kept thinking about it, and it wasn't until she internally processed what Yvette, Michael, and Sarah had said that she got why it made sense. Her comment "I figured out why!" had a note of triumph, and she eloquently showed why finding the area of the base and measuring the height in layers would work. This was a wonderful idea for Alicia, and opportunities to have those ideas are the essence of learning. As Eleanor Duckworth says,

> I see no difference in kind between wonderful ideas that many other people have already had, and wonderful ideas that nobody has yet happened upon. . . . The more we help children to have their wonderful ideas and feel

good about themselves for having them, the more likely it is that they will some day happen upon wonderful ideas that no one else has happened upon before. (1987a, 14)

Even though we had not written anything down, or taken notes, or solidified any of the ideas that had been offered, I decided to ask yet another question: If you were to find the volume of a cylinder, what information would you need? In our work with rectangular prisms, we had always related the dimensions (as length, width, and height) to the volume. I wondered how the students would think about "dimensions" in relation to cylinders. I called on Amy again, wanting her to be successful, and her answer was correct. Either height and radius or height and diameter would be sufficient to find the volume of a cylinder. At this point I made the decision to have the students consider a triangular prism—a different figure entirely—so as to continue with the notion of generalization. With a general principle in mind, students would be able to find the volume of any prism or cylinder as long as they could find the area of the base. The triangular prism query, an engaging question that produced a lot of raised hands, was a spontaneous idea prompted by a nearby index card that triggered for me the memory of an activity I used to do in which students folded index cards into the lateral surfaces of prisms and compared their volumes. Richard thought it was "easy." Usually I discourage the use of the word *easy* in my classes, because what is easy for one person can be mystifying for the next. And although it was apparent that he had been able to extend the idea of volume to this new figure, Richard struggled a bit in explaining how to find the area of the triangular base, making several mathematical errors in his explanation (showing that he would multiply the sides and divide it in half; talking about taking the length and width of the "square") that exposed some misconceptions about the area of a triangle. But one of a teacher's many decisions in discourse such as this is to decide "what to pursue in depth from among the ideas that students offer in discussions" (NCTM 1991, 35). I could tell that the general idea of volume made sense to him; we could address the triangle issue at another time and I didn't want those errors to derail the volume ideas under consideration. Then Sarah had another wonderful idea, making a connection that generalized volume for all right prisms and cylinders, and even as the bell rang, the students sat completely still.

After the students left, I pondered what had just happened. I most enjoy lessons in which my primary goal is to find out what students know so far and then engage their thinking about a mathematical idea that builds on their knowledge. I never know exactly where these lessons will go—what would I have done if Yvette had not connected the idea of rectangular prisms to cylinders? What if Sarah had not generalized for prisms and cylinders? In each of those cases, I would have needed to ask different questions and set different tasks for the students so that they would move toward the understandings they needed. Jim Greeno talks about the need for teachers to be able to walk around in the mathematical terrain under consideration, "getting from one location to another via a variety of routes" (in Hiebert et al. 1997, 35), and indeed, my third-period class took a different pathway toward the same mathematical goals. Deborah Ball (1993) discusses the tensions between representing content, respecting children as mathematical thinkers, and creating and using a community of mathematical discourse. These tensions had been in play for me in this lesson as I navigated the waters of using what students already understood to build new mathematical content knowledge through their mathematical community. There still was much work to be done; I had not assessed each student's understanding of the ideas that came under scrutiny, and students had not begun the task of building procedural fluency. But they had employed their capacities for logical thought, conjecture, and sense making to lay a foundation for the robust mathematical proficiency that I sought.

Case Commentary—Jo's Analysis

I wonder what students made of this lesson? It is common for teachers and researchers to watch lessons and consider the mathematical content that students may have learned. In this lesson the content was volume—specifically, finding the volume of prisms. Did students learn the mathematical method for finding the volume of prisms? It seems likely that they did, but the knowledge they did or did not gain is an inadequate representation of their learning. We did not videotape this lesson in order to investigate what the students would learn; that would have required a lot more than video, such as assessments of the mathematics and interviews with students. But it is interesting to consider the learning that was made available to students through the activities in which they engaged.

Connecting Mathematical Ideas

At an early point in the lesson, Cathy asked the students to make a *conjecture*. She held up a cylinder and asked them, "Is there anything about our rectangular prisms that could help us have a theory about how to find the volume of any of these?" In asking this question and gathering the different responses, Cathy and her students were *making connections*. They were connecting what they knew about the volume of rectangular prisms to what they knew about the dimensions of cylinders and extending their knowledge to produce a formula for finding the volume of a cylinder. It is important that students were producing a formula for the volume of a cylinder but it is also important that they were making such connections. When authors write textbooks and teachers plan lessons, they often isolate the different methods students need to know so that students can practice them in a focused way. But this can also strip mathematics of the connections that are at the heart of the subject. Students who work through long lists of isolated mathematical methods throughout their school careers do not know about drawing connections and when they enter situations when they would benefit from making connections or extending what they know to a new situation, it does not occur to them that they can do so (Boaler 1997, 2002b). When students were asked in this lesson, to draw connections, they were asked to engage in an important mathematical practice.

Visualizing

As the class moved through the lesson and students thought of ways to find the volume of a cylinder, they engaged in another practice that they had learned in Cathy's class—that of *visualization*. Michael started the process when she said that Yvette's suggestion to use a "regular circle" and multiply its area by the height of the cylinder would "make sense" because they had come up with a way of "visualizing . . . layers" when they had thought of rectangular prisms and "you would use the same thing for the cylinder." Alicia stated the idea most clearly, saying, "You're stacking the same area of the circle over and over again on top of itself." In my conversations with engineering professors at Stanford, reflecting upon the limits of students' mathematical preparations, they have told me that the ability that their students most lack is that of visualization. The practice of visualization is critical for engineers but it is also central to all of mathematical modeling. Visualization is part of being mathematical, yet it is rare to hear students discussing the process so naturally and vividly.

Extending Ideas

As students continued with their conversations, Cathy asked them to *justify* their thinking. It was not enough that students offered correct answers, saying that they should multiply the area of a circle by the height of the cylinder; Cathy asked them why that made sense. In their responses the students drew upon the norms of the discipline, offering visual representations to justify the formulas they offered. I was struck when watching this lesson by the fact that students were building upon each other's ideas and *extending* them. These are sophisticated acts of discourse that involve listening carefully to what others say and connecting them with new ideas (Schwartz 1999). Alicia illustrated this when she said: "It's . . . like Sarah's idea about the stacking of the little cubes," which she extended to a notion of stacking the area of a circle "over and over again." Such acts of listening to ideas and extending them are not often seen in classrooms (Barron 2003). It is common for students to work in groups in school but when their conversations are analyzed, observers frequently note that students do not often build upon each other's thinking; instead, they offer their own thoughts, disconnected from the conversation that preceded them. The act of listening to and extending ideas is important to classroom discourse as well as to the act of mathematics itself.

Generalizing

Another practice in which students engaged in this lesson extract was the act of *generalization*, which Sarah introduced and Cathy chose to highlight. Sarah said, "To find the volume of anything, what I . . . realized is that you have to find the area of just . . . a flat surface . . . so for the circle, [it is] just this circle . . . , then you need to multiply it by the height." Cathy highlighted this comment, asking students to note the act of generalization. She asked Sarah to expand on her comment, but the bell rang as Sarah was talking. What happened next is highly significant: the students did nothing. Not a single student spoke, packed away his or her belongings, or got ready to leave; there was no rustle of bags or shuffling in seats, no head turning or clock watching. The students were attending respectfully to Sarah's ideas. I have highlighted a number of mathematical events that took place in the short segment of class that we see; this act of respect also seems worthy of note.

Connections Between Mathematics and the World

At the beginning of the lesson, Cathy asked the students, "If you went into a grocery store, do you think you would find more things packaged in cylinders or more things packaged in boxes—rectangular prisms? I wonder." The students talked briefly and excitedly about this question, speculating as to what they would find. Cathy interjected with "I don't know. Now I'm curious" as the students talked. What happened in those brief moments at the beginning of the lesson? Some would say that time was wasted as the students were not learning new mathematical content. But Cathy was modeling something important: she was showing students that mathematics is all around them, that it is not an esoteric set of relationships removed from the realities of the world, but a way of interpreting and explaining the world. In those moments Cathy communicated a message that her students could be intrigued by the mathematical relationships in the world and that such curiosity is at the heart of mathematics.

Mathematical Practices

When I consider what students learned in this lesson, I think of mathematics knowledge but I also notice the different mathematical acts that I have described— making connections, visualizing, justifying, conjecturing, extending ideas, and generalizing. These are important acts, much like the acts of questioning, reasoning, and representing, which I highlighted in Chapter 6. All of these acts contribute to quantitative literacy (Steen 1997) and they lie at the heart of mathematical work, yet they are not content knowledge. In 2002 I was a member of a panel of mathematicians, mathematics educators, and psychologists, coordinated by RAND (2002), which had been given the task of outlining the most productive research directions in mathematics education for the future. One of the three research directions we proposed was that of "mathematical practices," a notion that was developed by Deborah Ball and Hyman Bass. The group described mathematical practices in the following way:

> This area focuses on the mathematical know-how, beyond content knowledge, that characterizes expertise in learning and using mathematics. The term "practices" refers to specific things that successful mathematics learners and users *do*. Justifying claims, using symbolic notation efficiently, and making generalizations are examples of mathematical practices. (Rand 2002, 29)

Mathematical practices are the repeated actions in which users of mathematics (as learners and problem solvers) engage. Take as an example the act of representation; the first thing many successful problem solvers do when they see a set of ideas in a question is represent them in some way, perhaps as a diagram, chart, or graph. The act of representing is an important mathematical practice but it is rarely taught. Students may be taught how to draw a chart or a graph, but knowing *when* to represent ideas with a graphic or schema is a different act that may or may not receive attention. The RAND panel described this as "representational sensibility," an awareness and consideration of what each form of representation makes most visible or best communicates. For example, one may consider whether a table, graph, or equation of a line makes the y-intercept or the rate of change most visible. Representational sensibility is a critical part of teachers' pedagogical content knowledge, as teachers frequently need to consider which representations give students the best access to ideas (Shulman 1986, 1987; Wilson 1992). It is also an aspect of general mathematical proficiency (Kilpatrick, Swafford, and Findell 2001). The following is a list of some of the mathematical practices we generated as part of our work on the RAND mathematics panel.

Exploration

- conjecturing/making a prediction
- guessing and checking
- trying an easier problem
- looking for patterns
- thinking in reverse/doing-undoing

Orienting and Organizing

- figuring out what the question is asking
- creating smaller problems to be solved
- establishing the *known* and the *unknown* in the problem
- asking, What kind of problem is it? What is similar or different about this problem?

Generalizing

- representing a mathematical relationship in more general terms (e.g., representing a rule or relationship using symbols, words, a graph)

Generalizing involves looking for rules and relationships and asking:

> What steps am I doing over and over again?
> What is changing?
> Do I have enough information to let me predict what will happen?
> Can I describe the steps I've been doing without using specific inputs?
> Does my rule only work for odd numbers?

Representing

Representing is part of both exploration (How can I make sense of this for myself?) and communication and justification (How can I explain/show/convince other people?). It involves

- drawing a picture or a diagram
- visualizing
- making a model
- using symbols
- verbalizing or putting into words
- rewording the problem

Checking for Appropriateness and Reasonableness

- Does my answer make sense in the context of the problem?
- Does my answer make sense in terms of my previous knowledge?

Connecting, Extending, Reconciling

- Will this rule work for other numbers?
- Can I use this process for a more general case?
- When is this rule true? Is it *always* true?
- For what systems of numbers or kinds of figures does it hold?
- Does previously held knowledge need to change?

Using Appropriate Mathematical Language

- creating and using definitions
- using mathematically precise and appropriate language
- using symbols correctly and appropriately
- having an awareness of mathematical conventions

Justifying

Justifying requires explaining, convincing, and proving, asking such questions as:

- Why does it work?
- How *sure* am I? Am I convinced?
- How can I represent the problem in such a way to make it convincing?
- What previously established knowledge do I draw on in making my case?
- What terms will I have to define in order to communicate my argument to others?
- Are explanations and proofs sufficiently convincing?

People who solve mathematics problems at any level need to engage in mathematical practices—similar in ways, to what NCTM (2000) calls processes—yet they are generally not taught. Indeed successful students learn to engage in these practices (through various experiences in and out of school) and unsuccessful students often do not. For that reason, the RAND mathematics panel related these practices to the achievement of equity. What would happen, we asked, if students were given more careful opportunity to learn these practices? Is it possible that careful teaching with awareness of mathematical practices (but not necessarily direct teaching of them) could reduce achievement gaps, making explicit what is often left implicit (White and Frederiksen 1998; Delpit 1988)? Contemplate any mathematical problem and consider how useful are the practices of, for example, trying out the problem with easier numbers, visualizing a solution, and representing the problem by creating a diagram or a graph. Such practices are honored in Cathy's teaching, as she engages students in explorations that require their use. In various clips we saw students representing mathematical concepts using diagrams and words; we see them justifying and convincing; we saw them connecting different methods; and we saw them learning to generalize. It is easy to imagine these students engaging in similarly important acts when they encounter other mathematical problems in later mathematics classes or in their lives outside of school. Students were learning mathematics knowledge in this lesson, but they were also learning to *act* mathematically.

Chapter 9

Surface Area
Generating Geometric Formulas (June 6)

Whenever possible, students should develop formulas and procedures
meaningfully through investigation rather than memorize them.

NCTM (2000, 244)

Background of the Lesson—Cathy's Perspective

Formulas, especially those involving pi, are often taught as "social" knowledge, or agreed-upon procedures (Kamii and Warrington 1999), rather than as relationships to understand. Consider, for example, the formula for the area of a circle, $A = \pi r^2$:

> Most of us first learned this formula in school with the justification that teacher said so, take it or leave it, but you better take it and learn it by heart; the formula is, in fact, an example of the brutality with which mathematics is often taught to the innocent. (Beckman 1971, 17)

While the word *brutality* may sound somewhat extreme, memorization of formulas without understanding contributes to the notion that mathematics is accessible only to the privileged few. *Principles and Standards for School Mathematics* states, "Even formulas that are difficult to justify rigorously in the middle grades, such as that for the area of a circle, should be treated in ways that help students develop an intuitive sense of their reasonableness" (NCTM 2000, 244). As we saw in Chapter 8, the students in this class had been able to use their hands-on experiences with rectangular prisms to make sense of formulas for the volume of prisms and cylinders. I wondered how their recent experiences with the flat patterns, or nets, of rectangular prisms might help them reason about the surface area of cylinders. The formula for the surface area of a cylinder is generally given as $SA = 2\pi r^2 + 2\pi rh$, where r is the radius of the base and h is the height of the cylinder. To many people, this formula looks incomprehensible. Why are the 2s there? Why does one term have an *h*? Why does one term have an r^2 while the other has only an *r*? These are questions I have always hoped students would wonder about, but over the years I have found that most students view this formula with dismay and wonder instead about how they will ever remember it.

Our text, *Filling and Wrapping* (Lappan et al. 1998a), suggests approaching this topic by providing the flat pattern for a cylinder on centimeter grid paper and then asking students to approximate its area. Next, teachers should instruct students to fold the flat pattern into a cylinder and relate the dimensions of the flat pattern to the dimensions of the cylinder; from this experience, students can draw conclusions about a general formula for surface area. I decided, however, that since one of the most interesting things about cylinders is what the flat pattern actually looks like, I didn't want to deprive students of an opportunity to think about this. Besides, approximating the area of a figure on grid paper would be trivial for them. So rather than handing out the flat pattern, I decided to start by challenging the students to figure out what the flat pattern of a cylinder would look like.

I was unsure, however, exactly where to go from there. How long would it take the students to agree on a generic flat pattern for a cylinder? Once they had agreed on what the net would look like, would they recognize its essential components? The day before, the students had thought about the dimensions of a cylinder in relation to volume; would this help them with its surface area? When working with the flat patterns of rectangular prisms, the students had had surprising difficulty relating the area of the flat pattern of a box they had cut apart to the surface area of the original box. Would this same disequilibrium emerge today? Should I engage students in deriving the formula? If so, how much should I guide them? My lesson plan for the day was full of questions.

I decided to trust my knowledge of both the mathematical terrain and of my students. Rather than covering the curriculum, I would allow the lesson to "uncover" (Hawkins, in Duckworth 1987, 7) what the students understood. I decided to listen closely and follow their lead.

Prior to the Video Selection

I gave each group scissors and a stack of paper from our recycling bin and posed the following question: "What do you think the flat pattern for a cylinder might look like?" All of the students became enthusiastically engaged in drawing, cutting, and experimenting, and there were many different versions of how the flat pattern might look. Their different ideas were fascinating and gave me a window into the difficulty of visualizing a three-dimensional figure in two dimensions. I had seen the same curiosity and persistence in Stanford preservice teachers to whom I had given the task of creating the net for an oblique circular cylinder. In both cases, most students, although initially unsuccessful, were relentless in their determination to figure it out. In order to honor their attempts, and curious about what they had tried, I asked, "Who tried something that didn't work?" Most students raised their hands, so I asked volunteers to go to the board and sketch what they had tried.

Why would I spend class time having students sketch incorrect patterns? For one thing, one of the biggest obstacles to mathematical investigation is the erroneous and dangerous notion that smart people don't take wrong turns in mathematics. Indeed, "tinkering" with ideas is a habit of mind employed regularly by mathematicians in the practice of their craft (Cuoco, Goldenberg, and Mark 1996). A joint endeavor such as this, where there are few preconceived notions, lends itself nicely to celebrating wrong answers. In addition, there was logic in each of these patterns, most of which contained kernels of what a correct flat pattern would look like. Finally, as we saw in Chapter 7, wrong answers were still viewed negatively by many of these students, despite my continuous efforts to build the notion of mistakes as sites for learning (Hiebert et al. 1997) into our class culture. Examining the patterns that didn't work provided one more opportunity to reinforce the important idea that wrong answers and confusion are not only normal but essential for learning.

The video selection begins as Jordan, who had enthusiastically tried several different ideas for flat patterns, was good-naturedly drawing another failed attempt on the board. See Figure 9–1.

Meanwhile, I noticed that several students had found flat patterns that worked. I got the students' attention and asked Crystal, who had made one of these, to hold her pattern up so everyone could see. (See Figure 9–2.)

As I glanced around the room, I saw that all of the correct patterns were in this configuration, with the circles directly opposite each other. Rather than focus the students' attention on other possible locations for the circles, I decided that it was more important to address the issue of the relative length of the rectangle. I asked Crystal how she had decided how long to make it, and Michael, who had

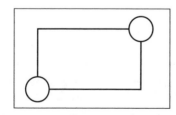

Figure 9–1.

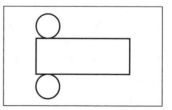

Figure 9–2.

worked with Crystal, said, "Guessed!" I referred my question to the class. "How long do you think this [pointing to the side of the rectangle on Crystal's net, which corresponded to the circumference of the circle] would need to be so it will wrap around the circle with no overlaps?" Artie conjectured that the rectangle looked about four times as long as the radius of the circle. Brittani, who had rarely made public conjectures, said she wasn't sure, but she held her flat pattern up and moved her hand around the circumference of one of the circles. Since Brittani's flat pattern was quite small, I asked her to use Crystal's larger flat pattern to demonstrate what she meant. This explanation is shown on the video.

Watch "Surface Area: Generating Geometric Formulas," CD 2

Lesson Analysis and Reflection

At the time Brittani stood up, most of the students had the general idea that the flat pattern consisted of a rectangle and two circles. But while most students had made rectangles that were too long and then folded any extra length underneath, Brittani and Evan had figured out that the length of the rectangle needed to be exactly as long as the circumference of the circle.

This was one of the first times all year that Brittani had enthusiastically shared her ideas with the class, and the fact that Evan, who was confident in his reasoning and enjoyed high mathematical status among his peers, built on her idea made this occurrence even more special. I wondered why this particular task had inspired such interest and confidence in Brittani; reflecting on this later, I was struck with how important it is to provide a wide variety of tasks so that every student has the opportunity to feel successful and smart. Teachers are currently under so much pressure to cover standards, and if these standards are primarily procedural, students may have precious little opportunity to develop the mathematical understandings, practices, and dispositions that build robust mathematical proficiency (Kilpatrick, Swafford, and Findell 2001).

I still wasn't sure if students could derive the formula for surface area, but since the essential attributes of the flat pattern had emerged from our discussion, I decided to let them give it a try. I drew a flat pattern matching Crystal's on the board and defined r as the length of the radius. Telling the class that I hadn't planned to ask them to try the following activity, and that I didn't know if they would be able to do it, I gave them the task of figuring out how to represent the length of the rectangle. Since this was precisely the relationship that Brittani and Evan had helped clarify, I was certain that the students could do this part, I just wasn't sure if they could generate the whole formula. I had never tried this with students before! In structuring it so they first represented the length of the rectangle, I was actually breaking the real problem—writing a formula for the surface area of the entire cylinder—into smaller parts. Afterward, I wondered if this had been a good decision. The words of one of my first mentors echo in my mind: "Say as little as you can without causing chaos." By this, she meant that the less we guide or direct, the more the children themselves will be doing the thinking. I wondered what would have happened if I had not defined the radius with a variable and given students the task of representing the length of the rectangle. Doing so probably helped the students find success within the confines of the time we had left, but it also deprived them of valuable complexity.

> [W]e organize subject matter into a neat series of steps which assumes a profound uniformity among students. We sand away at the interesting edges of subject matter until it is so free from its natural complexities, so neat, that there is not a crevice left as an opening. All that is left is to hand it to them, scrubbed and smooth, so that they can view it as outsiders. (L. Schneier in Duckworth 1991, 7)

I don't want students to be outsiders in their own learning, but on this day, in this lesson, I had made the decision to break the process down into smaller pieces. My time spent reflecting on the lesson has given me the opportunity to think about doing the lesson again with some other class, on some other day, in a different way to see what would happen.

Holly volunteered her idea about the length of the rectangle, saying, "Two radius times pi." She explained that this made sense because it was how you would find the circumference of the circle. I briefly considered pressing Holly about what the circumference of the circle had to do with the length of the rectangle but instead nodded and agreed because the class had just discussed this relationship. I knew that the tempo of the questioning was a little faster than normal and I was pressing for understanding less than usual. I hoped that these choices were not lessening the cognitive demand of the task (Stein et al. 2000), but in weighing the relative benefits of deeper questioning here versus having time to derive the formula, I opted for the latter.

The width of the rectangle—representing the height of the can—was the next issue to address. I decided to ask the students whether they needed another variable or not as a natural extension of work they had done during the previous unit, when they had grappled with the issue of dependence (I had asked this same question on the second day of that unit in a class discussion captured in Chapter 3). The students were still interested in this question, which is not trivial, and I was on the verge of giving them time for small-group discussions. Instead, for the same reasons discussed earlier, I decided to ask if anyone could present an argument for using an additional variable. I called on Pirmin because he rarely volunteered in whole-class discussions. (This was a great day for different students volunteering! I wonder whether it was the visual nature of the task or whether it had anything to do with the discussion we had had about class discussions, a few days earlier?) Pirmin answered that the width of the rectangle could be "any distance because it doesn't have to wrap around anything . . . it's just how much you want to put in the can." I always try hard to listen to what students are really saying rather than listening for what I want to hear. But, from my knowledge of the work we had done in the last unit as well as my knowledge of Pirmin, I knew that when he said "any distance," he meant the width of the rectangle was not *dependent* on the length of the radius; his further justification, that "it's just how much you want to put in the can," related the width of the rectangle to the three-dimensional context of the original problem. I could certainly have pressed him to be more clear about these relationships, though!

One of the most seductive traps a teacher can fall into is to assume that once a correct answer has been publicly stated (either by a student or by the teacher), it has become common knowledge. I knew that not everyone understood what Pirmin was talking about, nor did everyone now agree that another variable was needed. But I validated his answer rather than pressing the students to do so. This was another unusual decision for me. At another time in the year I probably would have taken the opportunity to dig into this more deeply in order to make sure that everyone could explain to him- or herself why another variable was needed. We had, however, just finished a unit on algebraic representation during which students had had to grapple with this very issue, and I was pretty sure that most students knew that if the height was not related to the width, they would need another variable for the height. I trusted that the collaborative class culture that we had been building all year would enable disagreements or clarifications to arise in small groups rather than in the whole-class setting.

I said that I wanted them "to figure out a formula to find the surface area of [the flat pattern drawn on the board]." This language was not precisely correct; there is a difference between finding the *area* of a flat pattern and finding a formula for the *surface area* of a three-dimensional object, even though the answers are the same. When I had started this unit, I thought this relationship would be obvious. One of my favorite sayings, "'Obvious' is the most dangerous word in mathematics" (Bell 1951, 16), also applies to mathematics *teaching*. What is clearly apparent to us is so often mystifying to our students. But in this case, since the class had already addressed this issue with rectangular prisms, most students knew what I meant even though I had not said it quite right.

They got involved quickly and worked together enthusiastically to figure out a formula. Many students struggled with the idea of using variables as measurements because it was the first time they had done this. But it was interesting for them; it seemed challenging and they liked that. Could they do it? I was betting that they could, and I could see that they thought they could, too. In a matter of minutes, most groups had made significant progress toward deriving the formula, and some, like Leslie, Jordan, Holly, and Zach, indeed had it. As they went to the overhead projector to reveal their formula, their pride and enthusiasm was evident.

There were only five minutes remaining in the class period; we had no time for more ways to think about the formula or for questioning Leslie's group. Then someone asked, "Do we have to memorize it?" (to the accompaniment of widespread moans). Although this question was so typical of seventh graders, I also found it amazing and amusing. They had just derived the formula for the surface area of a cylinder and they were worried about memorizing it? They didn't realize how mathematically powerful they were! I used this comment as an opportunity to say, one last time, what I knew about them: that if they had figured it out one time, they could do it again. One of my favorite quotations comes to mind:

> What you are obliged to discover for yourself leaves a path in your mind which you can use again when the need arises. (Lichtenberg)

Case Commentary—Jo's Analysis

In the last chapter, I wrote about the mathematical ways of working that were being developed in the volume lesson. In this lesson we again saw students engaged in various mathematical practices, such as representation, visualization, and generalization, but we also saw Cathy encouraging a particular *orientation* toward knowledge. In my own studies of students learning mathematics in England and the United States, fellow researchers and I have observed that different teaching approaches encourage very different relationships with the discipline of mathematics, and that such relationships, or orientations, are extremely important (Boaler 2002a, 2002b; Gresalfi, Boaler, and Cobb 2004). When people consider the value of different mathematics teaching approaches, they tend to evaluate the *amount* of knowledge students hold and can demonstrate on tests. But students do not only learn knowledge in mathematics classrooms; they also develop a relationship with the domain that will impact their use of mathematics for the rest of their lives.

Orientations Toward Knowledge

Jim Greeno and I wrote about a study in which Megan Staples and I interviewed students in AP calculus classes (Boaler and Greeno 2000). Some of the students experienced a traditional approach to calculus in which they listened to the teacher explain methods and then practiced them. Other students experienced an approach that involved discussing different methods and considering the connections between them. The students gave very clear indications that such approaches encouraged different orientations toward their mathematics knowledge. Two positions we identified were those of "received" and "connected" knowing (Belencky et al. 1986, 35). In the position of received knowing, students were required to engage in passive learning practices, such as paying careful attention and reproducing what the teachers showed them. The students reported that there was no room for their own ideas or for them to use their own "agency," and for many this passive positioning turned them away from mathematics. Those who were happy being positioned as received knowers were those who wanted to just absorb or develop knowledge without questioning or exploring interpretations. For example, one student told us, "I don't really think about how or why something is the way it is. I just like math because it is or it isn't" (Jerry, Lemon School) (Boaler and Greeno 2000, 185). In other classes in which students were expected to form connections and to reason, offering their own ideas and thoughts in the resolution of mathematical conflicts, students were given the opportunity to engage in a form of connected knowing (Belencky et. al. 1986, 100). Contrast the position communicated by Jerry earlier, with that communicated by a student in our recent study, who was learning in a more open environment:

> If nothing else, it's just breaking out of the pattern of just taking something that's given to you and accepting it and just, you know, going with it. Like political things that happen and, you know, media things. It's just looking at it and you try and point yourself in a different angle and look at it and reinterpret it. So, you know, it's the same thing. It's like if you have this set of data that you need to look at to find an answer to, you know, if people just go at it one way straightforward you might hit a wall. But there might be a crack somewhere else that you can fit through and get into the meaty part. (Ernie, IMP 4)

These two students do not just communicate different beliefs about mathematics but different positions toward knowledge that are highly likely to impact the way they approach mathematics problems in the future. Whereas Jerry likes to be told the way things are, and not think about it, Ernie talks about his willingness to interpret data and consider mathematical situations from different angles. He talks explicitly about a form of quantitative literacy (Steen 1997) when he says that he would question "political things" and "media things," considering different interpretations of mathematical data. It seems clear that Ernie is developing a more productive orientation toward mathematical knowledge.

These different positionings are important for at least two reasons. First, the positions available to students impact their enjoyment of mathematics. Many of the students who were required to act as received knowers in our calculus study told us that they resented such passive engagement. Despite their high-level performance and success in mathematics, they told us that they would cease taking mathematics classes as soon as possible. At Stanford I have had many conversations with students who were extremely mathematically able but chose to pursue majors in subjects such as engineering or computer science rather than mathematics, because the professors of these subjects gave them opportunities to use their own ideas, discuss different methods, and act with agency. It seems that the passive engagement often offered to students in mathematics classrooms turns many of them away from high-level mathematical work. The students who engaged in connected knowing practices in our calculus study were more positive about both mathematics and their future in the discipline.

Extending Mathematical Ideas

In addition to affecting the enjoyment students gain from different classroom practices, the relationships students are offered impact their use of mathematics in life. Students who learn only to accept or receive standard methods do not think they can adapt or extend mathematical methods, as they have never taken such an active part in their mathematical work. When faced with mathematics problems in their lives, they often feel paralyzed as they strive unsuccessfully to remember the appropriate method (Boaler 2002b). Students who have engaged more actively in mathematics classes are often more successful because they can build from ideas without remembering precise methods. Cathy encouraged such a stance toward mathematics in this lesson when she said; "If you ever needed to be able to find the surface area of a cylinder for some reason . . . you don't have to say, 'oh what's the formula? Give me my book, [I'll] look it up.' You can say, 'Wait a second, I can figure this out, I have enough information.'" In addition to communicating the message that students *could* solve mathematical problems by thinking carefully, Cathy required them to do so. She asked students to figure out a formula for surface area; this showed them that such a formula could be derived and gave them a general awareness that they could use their own ideas and the mathematical practices that they had learned in class to solve problems. In this class period we did not see students being positioned as received knowers; we saw them being asked to problem solve, to adapt and extend methods, to derive formulas, and to engage in critical thinking. Such actions offer students an important positive orientation toward mathematical knowledge.

Engaging in Authentic Mathematical Work

Some people believe that students should not receive the opportunity to problem solve or derive methods, acting in similar ways to research mathematicians (Burton 1999), until they reach graduate school; they think that K–12 schools should just instill all the methods and formulas that students will need for later study. But by delaying students' experiences with authentic mathematical work (Lampert 1990; Cobb et al. 1997), we turn many students away from the discipline, and many capable and creative thinkers who used to enjoy mathematics (Boaler and Greeno 2000) choose to study other areas. There are many reasons to pay attention to the orientations students develop toward mathematics; in the surface area case we witnessed Cathy acting quite deliberately to encourage an active and authentic form of participation and orientation.

Maintaining a Small Inferential Gap

Teaching takes place at a particular point in time and viewers of a case can never know all that has gone on before. In this case we got a clear sense of the time of the year as Cathy talked to students about the limited opportunities she would have to talk with them after "this week." Indeed, this lesson took place on the last day of class. The place of this lesson in the year seemed evident as we witnessed a slightly faster pace to the lesson and a slight shift in Cathy's method of questioning. I have talked about the importance of teacher questions and the need for questions that ask students for different types of mathematical thinking and understanding (see Chapter 3). Another critical part of the questioning process concerns the decisions teachers make regarding whether to follow up on what students have said or to "press" (Kazemi 1998) for further clarification of ideas. Staples (2004) studied a teacher who was particularly successful at establishing communities of students who discussed ideas. She noted that an important part of the teacher's practice was that of maintaining a very small "inferential gap"; that is, she always followed up with students until they gave complete and clear explanations of the ideas they were communicating. Staples described this practice as follows:

> One example of Ms. Nelson's use of this small inferential gap is her *press* for clear articulation of ideas. Certainly one goal of her press was making one student's thinking available to other students. But her press was also guided by her reluctance to make assumptions about a student's level of understanding based on a partial articulation. Rather, she kept open the question of understanding, often choosing to gather further evidence about the students' understanding. In this way, she held very high standards for what counted as evidence of understanding as well as the level of clarity students needed to reach in articulating their ideas. (253)

The different cases that make up this collection show Cathy maintaining a small inferential gap when she questions students, making sure that they have given full and clear explanations before she moves on. In this extract we saw a slightly larger gap than was evident in many of her lessons. Viewers may notice that she asked Pirmin if the class needed another variable to write the formula. He answered, "Basically, that could be any distance because it doesn't have to wrap around anything." Cathy checked on some of his statement, then said "So it can be as high as you want it to be. So the answer is yes, you do need another variable." In this instance Cathy left a small gap between what Pirmin said—that the distance could be any length—and her conclusion that another variable was needed. Most viewers would conclude that Pirmin was indicating that another variable was needed, but a small gap is evident nonetheless. In other instances when Cathy questioned students, she did not leave any inferential gap, pressing the students to fully articulate what they meant. When a teacher presses a student to articulate her thinking, it benefits the student-teacher interaction because the student's understanding is monitored and the teacher gets a clearer opportunity to help the student, but it also benefits the rest of the class because other students are given the opportunity to hear well-articulated mathematical reasoning.

Using Correct Terminology

In addition to full articulation, Cathy requires that students are precise in their use of mathematical terminology and their naming of variables. She models for students the correct language to use, and she insists that they use correct terminology themselves. In this case we saw instances of Cathy telling students about the correct way to write an expression. For example, she told them that they should put pi before the variable because it was a number, and later on she asked Leslie to correct her naming of the rectangle as a "box." Cathy is similar to the teacher in the Staples (2004) study, as they both go to great pains to insist upon correct terminology and labeling. This is interesting because both teachers would identify themselves as reform oriented, and lack of precision is one of the arguments that is often leveled against reform-oriented approaches. There seems to be a number of ideas communicated about reform teaching that are less than accurate, such as the idea that reform teaching is student centered and traditional teaching is teacher centered. Few would watch these cases of teaching and think that Cathy was not central to the students' work. But Cathy's centrality does not mean that students are not allowed to think; indeed, her centrality is enacted in the service of encouraging students' thinking. It seems that the idea that teachers are less involved in discussion-oriented approaches is ill informed. Observers of the traditional classes we are studying in our National Science Foundation (NSF) project have been struck by the lack of teacher input, with students spending the vast majority of their time interacting only with the textbook. If we value mathematical precision and the correct use of terminology, then approaches in which teachers have opportunities to model and encourage the use of correct terminology should be encouraged.

This is the last of the cases we present and the last substantive lesson in the year, so it seems appropriate to consider some of the norms (Yackel and Cobb 1996; McClain and Cobb 2001) that Cathy developed across the year and that we saw in place in this lesson. Cobb and his colleagues distinguish between norms that are social and those that are mathematical. Social norms concern actions such as listening to other students and showing respect for each other. Such norms are critical for classes in which discussions are encouraged. Other norms are defined as sociomathematical, because they are partly social (they involve communication between people) but they are also intrinsically mathematical. An example of a sociomathematical norm would be the amount of mathematical justification that a teacher requires students to give (McClain and Cobb 2001).

Social Norms

In all of the cases we saw the students discussing different ideas carefully and respectfully. This did not come about because the students were particularly advanced but because of the deliberate and consistent work of the teacher. In all of the lessons Cathy encouraged the different practices that go into collaborative work, such as offering ideas, listening carefully, building upon ideas, and respecting each other. Cathy encouraged these norms in many different ways. She encouraged students to share their ideas by telling them that all ideas—correct and incorrect—were valuable, as they all provided insights for learning. Many of the students reflected in the end-of-year interviews that this was the first mathematics class they had experienced in which they had felt it was acceptable to have wrong answers. Victor said in his interview, "Being wrong is what learning is all about; it is really the only way to learn, because someone could teach it to you but then you might not . . . you have to experience it yourself, like, 'Ohhh I get it now.'" Alicia added, "If you are not open to being wrong, then you don't really learn." Cathy encouraged listening by asking students to listen carefully and to keep their hands down when others were speaking. She encouraged them to build upon each other's ideas by frequently asking questions such as "what do you think about what Alicia just said?" We saw the impact of such encouragement in the surface area case when Evan listened to Brittani's explanation and then said, "I agree with Brittani because this part right here that goes around it, it has to be able to go from here all the way around and back to here." This action of building upon another student's idea is, in many ways, the most noteworthy part of collaboration and the most difficult to achieve. When a student builds upon the ideas of another, she is not only thinking about the ideas put forward but constructing a representation of another person's thoughts (Schwartz 1999).

Sociomathematical Norms

Schwartz (1999) tells us that an advanced form of collaboration is seen when students move beyond the act of *communication* to the goal of *mutual understanding*. In some classrooms students communicate with each other by sharing ideas, but a concern for mutual understanding means that students are doing more—they are actively working to help others understand. I saw evidence of this shift in Cathy's classes and it seems clear that students benefit from the work their fellow students do to communicate ideas carefully and in different ways. Two particular mathematical practices are critical to the development of mutual understanding: justification and representation. The act of justification is important to mathematical work. It is also a significant aid to learning. Every time Cathy asks her students, "And why does that make sense?" she is asking them to justify their thinking. When students engage in justification they are articulating their ideas and interacting with the teacher and other students around them. They are also providing important support to other students who may not understand where particular ideas have come from. In other studies of teachers who have been particularly successful at eliminating achievement gaps and promoting equity, I have noted the important role played by justification (Boaler 2004). When students justify their thinking they help themselves learn and provide a support to others.

The other practice that is valuable in the development of mutual understanding is that of representation (see also Chapter 6). Across the different cases we saw a number of different instances when students offered representations of ideas to help communicate important qualities of a concept or method. In the fraction case Sam went to the board and illustrated the division of fractions using a pie chart. Then Evan followed him to the board and illustrated the same idea using a line diagram. In the second part of the proof case, we saw Colin representing ideas using algebra and Melissa representing similar concepts using a graphic diagram. As different students went to the board and showed different representations we heard appreciative oohs and aahs and exclamations of "I get it." In the surface area case, we saw students representing cylinders through the construction of nets, or flat patterns. The act of representing is extremely helpful in communicating ideas and supporting mutual understanding; it is also a critical process for individuals to learn so that they may capture, edit, and create ideas with fluency (Eisner 2004).

Tackling Complex Problems

Another important norm of Cathy's classroom concerns the tackling of difficult and complex problems. Consider the problem she gave students in this case—representing a cylinder on a plane and generating the formula for its surface area.

This is a difficult task, especially for young students early in their mathematical careers, yet the students attacked the task with some gusto and enthusiasm. In this lesson Cathy had adapted the task offered in the curriculum guide, as she wrote about in her lesson notes. She opened the task, requiring the students to do more, in order to provide them with additional learning experiences and opportunities for high-level thinking (Stein et al. 2000). In Staples' study of a highly successful teacher, she also found that the teacher frequently engaged in task adaptation. This practice is likely to be characteristic of good teachers more generally.

Connecting Geometric and Algebraic Representations

Another important characteristic of the work performed by Cathy's students is the fluid movement between algebraic and geometric representations. In this case, Cathy asked the students whether they needed another variable to express a formula for the surface area of a cylinder. Such a question directly connects algebraic and geometric representation—and reminds us of the second part of the Border Problem case, when Cathy asked the same important question. In the second part of the proof case, we saw students move between algebraic and geometric understanding as they communicated their reasoning for the equivalence of $2(n-1)$ and $2n-2$.

In the final moments of the surface area case, one of the students asked if the class would have to memorize the formula for the surface area of a cylinder. Some will be disappointed that students asked this question and pleased by Cathy's response. I was encouraged by the question, because it reflects some important thinking. Learners of mathematics need to consider which of the methods they learn are important to memorize and which can be derived through thought. In my studies of students learning mathematics, spanning more than ten years, I have found that many students believe that they have to memorize everything and such a perspective causes students trouble when they encounter mathematics problems. The student asking the question in this lesson showed an appreciation that there are some methods that do not have to be memorized, demonstrating a more nuanced understanding of the mathematical domain.

—

This is the final case that Cathy and I present and explore. We hope that you have enjoyed the book and the accompanying cases and that they have provided sites for investigation and inquiry. Part of our aim in producing this set of cases has been to present some of the complexity of teaching. The detailed intellectual work evident in the lessons and Cathy's written reflections is representative of the task of teaching, yet teaching is rarely presented as a complicated, intellectual act in public discussions. There is a prevailing view in society that anyone who knows something can teach it. We hope that this book presents a more realistic account of the work and the thinking involved (Lampert 1998). Cathy and I have unpacked some of the teaching decisions and moves that go into teaching in order to consider different elements of the practice and in the hope of adding to an important genre of work. Teachers' own accounts of their work, such as those provided by Deborah Ball (1993), Magdalene Lampert (1985, 2001), and Vivian Paley (1990, 1993), give fascinating and realistic insights into the demands of the teaching act. Such accounts of teaching pave an important path for others to tread—both in revealing the nature of teaching in ways that it has not previously been revealed and in providing a resource for inquiring teachers who want to enrich their own practice. We hope that this book and the accompanying cases have provided a similar resource and that may inspire other teachers to share their craft, so that others may learn from the practice of teaching.

References

Ball, D. L. 1993. "With an Eye on the Mathematical Horizon: Dilemmas of Teaching Elementary Mathematics." *The Elementary School Journal* 93 (4): 373–97.

Ball, D., and H. Bass. 2000. "Bridging Practices: Intertwining Content and Pedagogy in Teaching and Learning to Teach." In *Multiple Perspectives on Mathematics Teaching and Learning*, ed. J. Boaler, 83–104. Westport, CT: Ablex.

Ball, D., and D. Cohen. 1999. "Developing Practice, Developing Practitioners." In *Teaching as the Learning Profession: Handbook on Policy and Practice*, eds. L. Darling-Hammond and H. Sykes, San Francisco: Jossey–Bass.

Barron, B. 2003. "When Smart Groups Fail." *The Journal of the Learning Sciences* 12 (3): 307–59.

Beck, T. A. 1998. "Are There Any Questions? One Teacher's View of Students and Their Questions in a Fourth-Grade Classroom." *Teaching and Teacher Education* 14 (8): 871–86.

Beckman, P. 1971. *A History of (Pi)*. New York: St. Martin's.

Belencky, M. F., B. M. Clinchy, N. R. Goldberger, and J. M. Tarule. 1986. *Women's Ways of Knowing: The Development of Self, Voice and Mind*. New York: Basic.

Bell, E. T. 1951. *Mathematics: Queen and Servant of Science*. Washington, DC: Mathematical Association of America.

Black, P., and D. Wiliam. 1998. "Inside the Black Box: Raising Standards Through Classroom Assessment." *Phi Delta Kappan* (October): 139–48.

Boaler, J. 1997. *Experiencing School Mathematics: Teaching Styles, Sex and Setting*. Buckingham, PA: Open University Press.

———. 2000. "Mathematics from Another World: Traditional Communities and the Alienation of Learners." *Journal of Mathematical Behavior* 18 (4): 379–97.

———. 2002a. "The Development of Disciplinary Relationships: Knowledge, Practice and Identity in Mathematics Classrooms." *For the Learning of Mathematics* 22 (1): 42–47.

———. 2002b. *Experiencing School Mathematics: Traditional and Reform Approaches to Teaching and Their Impact on Student Learning*. Rev. and exp. ed. Mahwah, NJ: Lawrence Erlbaum.

———. 2003a. "Equitable Teaching Practices: The Case of Railside." Plenary presentation at the California Mathematics Conference, Asilomar, CA.

———. 2003b. "When Learning No Longer Matters: Standardized Testing and the Creation of Inequality." *Phi Delta Kappan* 84 (7): 502–6.

———. 2004. *Promoting Equity in Mathematics Classrooms—Important Teaching Practices and Their Impact on Student Learning*. Regular Lecture given at ICME, Copenhagen, Denmark.

Boaler, J., and K. Brodie. 2004. "The Importance of Depth and Breadth in the Analysis of Teaching: A Framework for Analysing Teacher Questions." Paper presented at the Psychology of Mathematics Education NA, Toronto, Ontario.

Boaler, J., and J. Greeno. 2000. "Identity, Agency and Knowing in Mathematics Worlds." In *Multiple Perspectives on Mathematics Teaching and Learning*, ed. J. Boaler, 171–200. Westport, CT: Ablex.

Bolster, A. S. 1983. "Toward a More Effective Model of Research on Teaching." *Harvard Educational Review* 53 (3): 294–308.

Booth, L. 1988. "Children's Difficulties in Beginning Algebra." In *The Ideas of Algebra, K–12*, eds. A. Coxford and A. Shulte, 20–32. Reston, VA: National Council of Teachers of Mathematics.

Bouvier, A. 1987. "The Right to Make Mistakes." *For the Learning of Mathematics* 7 (3): 17–25.

Bransford, J., A. Brown, and R. Cocking. 1999. *How People Learn: Brain, Mind, Experience and School*. Washington, DC: National Academy Press.

Brenner, M. E., R. E. Mayer, B. Moseley, T. Brar, R. Durán, B. S. Reed, and D. Webb. 1997. "Learning by Understanding: The Role of Multiple Representations in Learning Algebra." *American Educational Research Journal* 34: 663–89.

Brown, C. A., T. P. Carpenter, V. L. Kouba, M. M. Lindquist, E. A. Silver, and J. O. Swafford. 1988. "Secondary School Results for the Fourth NAEP Mathematics Assessment: Algebra, Geometry, Mathematical Methods, and Attitudes." *Mathematics Teacher* 81: 337–47.

Brown, R. G., M. P. Dolciani, R. H. Sorgenfrey, and W. L. Cole. 2000. *Algebra: Structure and Method*. Evanston, IL: McDougal Littel.

Burns, M. 1995. *Writing in Math Class*. White Plains, NY: Math Solutions.

Burns, M., and C. Humphreys. 1990. *A Collection of Math Lessons for Grades 6–8*. White Plains, NY: Math Solutions.

Burton, L. 1999. "The Practices of Mathematicians: What Do They Tell Us About Coming to Know Mathematics?" *Educational Studies in Mathematics* 37: 121–43.

California State Department of Education. 1987. *Mathematics Model Curriculum Guide: Kindergarten Through Grade Eight*. Sacramento, CA: California State Department of Education.

Carpenter, T., M. Franke, and L. Levi. 2003. *Thinking Mathematically: Integrating Arithmetic and Algebra in Elementary School.* Portsmouth, NH: Heinemann.

Chazan, D. 2000. *Beyond Formulas in Mathematics and Teaching: Dynamics of the High School Algebra Classroom.* New York: Teachers College Press.

Chazan, D., and D. L. Ball. 1999. "Beyond Being Told Not to Tell." *For the Learning of Mathematics* 9: 2–10.

Ciardello, A. V. 2000. "Student Questioning and Multidimensional Literacy in the Twenty-First Century." *The Educational Forum* 64: 215–22.

Cobb, P., A. Boufi, K. McClain, and J. Whitenack. 1997. "Reflective Discourse and Collective Reflection." *Journal for Research in Mathematics Education* 28 (3): 258–77.

Cuoco, A., E. Goldenberg, and J. Mark. 1996. "Habits of Mind: An Organizing Principle for Mathematics Curricula." *Journal of Mathematical Behavior* 15: 375–402.

Davidson, A., and P. Phelan. 1999. "Students' Multiple Worlds: An Anthropological Approach to Understanding Students' Engagement with School." In *Advances in Motivation and Achievement: Role of Context,* vol II, 233–83. Stamford, CT: JAI.

Delpit, L. 1988. "The Silenced Dialogue: Power and Pedagogy in Educating Other People's Children." *Harvard Educational Review* 58 (3): 280–98.

Demana, F., and J. Leitzel. 1988. "Establishing Fundamental Concepts Through Numerical Problem Solving." In *The Ideas of Algebra, K–12,* eds. A. Coxford and A. Shulte, 61–68. Reston, VA: National Council of Teachers of Mathematics.

Dossey, J. 1997. "Making Algebra Dynamic and Motivating: A National Challenge." In *The Nature and Role of Algebra in the K–14 Curriculum: Proceedings of a National Symposium,* 37–40. Washington, DC: National Academy Press.

Driscoll, M. 1999. *Fostering Algebraic Thinking: A Guide for Teachers Grades 6–10.* Portsmouth, NH: Heinemann.

Duckworth, E. 1987a. "The Having of Wonderful Ideas." In *"The Having of Wonderful Ideas" and Other Essays on Teaching and Learning,* 1–14. New York: Teachers College Press.

———. 1987b. "The Virtues of Not Knowing." In *"The Having of Wonderful Ideas" and Other Essays on Teaching and Learning,* 64–69. New York: Teachers College Press.

———. 1987c. "Teaching and Research." In *"The Having of Wonderful Ideas" and Other Essays on Teaching and Learning,* 122–40. New York: Teachers College Press.

———. 1991. "Twenty-Four, Forty-Two, and I Love You: Keeping It Complex." *Harvard Educational Review* 61 (1): 1–23.

Eisner, E. 1998. *The Kind of Schools We Need: Personal Essays.* Portsmouth, NH: Heinemann.

———. 2004. "Preparing for Today and Tomorrow." *Educational Leadership* (January): 7–10.

Erikson, F. 1996. "Going for the Zone: The Social and Cognitive Ecology of Teacher-student Interactions in Classroom Settings." In *Discourse, Learning and Schooling*, ed. D. Hicks, 29–62. Cambridge: Cambridge University Press.

Fendel, D., D. Resek, with L. Alper, and S. Fraser. 1997. *Interactive Mathematics Program: Year 1*. Emeryville, CA: Key Curriculum.

Fiori, N. 2004. "Refining Math Through Teacher Education." Unpublished paper. Stanford, CA: Stanford University.

Frank, M. L. 1988. "Problem Solving and Mathematical Beliefs." *Arithmetic Teacher* (January) 35 (5): 32–34.

Fredricks, J., P. Blumenfeld, and A. Paris. 2004. "School Engagement: Potential of the Concept, State of the Evidence." *Review of Educational Research* 74: 59–109.

Gainsburg, J. 2003. *The Mathematical Behavior of Structural Engineers*. Stanford, CA: Stanford University, Dissertation Abstracts International, A 64/05.

Gilbert, M. 2001. "Applying the Equity Principle." *Mathematics Teaching in the Middle School* 7 (1): 18–19, 36.

Good, T. L., R. L. Slavings, H. K. Hobseon, and H. Emerson. 1987. "Student Passivity: A Study of Question Asking in K–12 Classrooms." *Sociology of Education* 60 (July): 181–99.

Greeno, J. G. 1991. "Number Sense as Situated Knowing in a Conceptual Domain." *Journal for Research in Mathematics Education* 22 (3): 170–218.

Gresalfi, M., J. Boaler, and P. Cobb. 2004. "Exploring an Elusive Link Between Knowledge and Practice: Students' Disciplinary Orientations." Paper presented at the Psychology of Mathematics Education NA, Toronto, Ontario.

Haimes, D. 1996. "The Implementation of a 'Function' Approach to Introductory Algebra: A Case Study of Teacher Cognitions, Teacher Actions, and the Intended Curriculum." *Journal for Research in Mathematics Education* 27: 582–602.

Hiebert, J. 1999. "Relationships Between Research and the NCTM Standards." *Journal for Research in Mathematics Education* 31 (1): 3–19.

Hiebert, J., T. Carpenter, E. Fennema, K. Fuson, D. Wearne, H. Murray, et al. 1997. *Making Sense: Teaching and Learning Mathematics with Understanding*. Portsmouth, NH: Heinemann.

Hiebert, J., and D. Wearne. 1993. "Interactional Tasks, Classroom Discourse, and Students' Learning in Second-Grade Arithmetic." *American Educational Research Journal* 30 (2): 393–425.

Hollar, J., and K. N. Norwood. 1999. "The Effects of a Graphing-Approach Intermediate Algebra Curriculum on Students' Understanding of Function." *Journal for Research in Mathematics Education* 30: 220–26.

Howden, H. 1990. "Prior Experiences." In *Algebra For Everyone*, ed. E. Edwards, 7–23. Reston, VA: National Council of Teachers of Mathematics.

Hufferd-Ackles, K., K. Fuson, and M. G. Sherin. 2004. "Describing Levels and Components of a Math-talk Community." *Journal for Research in Mathematics Education* 35 (2): 81–116.

Humphreys, C. 2000. "Building Understanding of Algebraic Representation: A Unit for Seventh Grade." Master's writing project, San Jose State University.

Kamii, C., and M. Warrington. 1999. "Teaching Fractions: Fostering Children's Own Reasoning." In *Developing Mathematical Reasoning in Grades K–12*, 82–92. Reston, VA: National Council of Teachers of Mathematics.

Kazemi, E. 1998. "Discourse That Promotes Conceptual Understanding." *Teaching Children Mathematics* (March), 410–14.

Kieran, C. 1992. "The Learning and Teaching of School Algebra." In *Handbook of Research on Mathematics Teaching and Learning*, ed. D. A. Grouws, 390–419. New York: Macmillan. 390–419.

Kieran, C., and L. Chalouh. 1993. "Prealgebra: The Transition from Arithmetic to Algebra." In *Research Ideas for the Classroom: Middle Grades Mathematics*, ed. D. Owens, 179–98. New York: Macmillan.

Kilpatrick, J., J. Swafford, and B. Findell, eds. 2001. *Adding It Up: Helping Children Learn Mathematics*. Washington, DC: National Academy Press.

Kolata, G. 1997. "Understanding the News." In *Why Numbers Count: Quantitative Literacy for Tomorrow's America*, ed. L. A. Steen, 23–29. New York: College Entrance Examination Board.

Lakatos, I. 1976. *Proofs and Refutations*. Cambridge: Cambridge University Press.

Lampert, M. 1985. "How Do Teachers Manage to Teach? Perspectives on Problems in Practice." *Harvard Educational Review* 55 (2): 178–94.

———. 1990. "When the Problem Is Not the Question and the Solution Is Not the Answer: Mathematical Teaching and Learning." *American Educational Research Journal* 27 (1): 29–63.

———. 1998. "Studying Teaching as a Thinking Practice." In *Thinking Practices in Mathematics and Science Learning*, eds. J. G. Greeno and S. Goldman, 53–78. Mahwah, NJ: Lawrence Erlbaum.

———. 2001. *Teaching Problems and the Problems of Teaching*. New Haven, CT: Yale University Press.

Lappan, G., J. Fey, W. Fitzgerald, S. Friel, and E. Phillips. 1998a. *Filling and Wrapping*. Menlo Park, CA: Dale Seymour.

———. 1998b. *Say It with Symbols*. Menlo Park, CA: Dale Seymour.

———. 1998c. *Bits and Pieces I*. Menlo Park, CA: Dale Seymour.

———. 1998d. *Bits and Pieces II*. Menlo Park, CA: Dale Seymour.

———. 1998e. *Comparing and Scaling*. Menlo Park, CA: Dale Seymour.

———. 1998f. *Covering and Surrounding*. Menlo Park, CA: Dale Seymour.

———. 1998g. *Data About Us*. Menlo Park, CA: Dale Seymour.

———. 1998h. *How Likely Is It?*. Menlo Park, CA: Dale Seymour.

———. 1998i. *Prime Time*. Menlo Park, CA: Dale Seymour.

———. 1998j. *Stretching and Shrinking*. Menlo Park, CA: Dale Seymour.

———. 1998k. *Shapes and Designs*. Menlo Park, CA: Dale Seymour.

Lave, J. 1988. *Cognition in Practice*. Cambridge: Cambridge University Press.

Lee, L. 1996. "An Initiation into Algebraic Culture Through Generalization Activities." In *Approaches to Algebra: Perspectives for Teaching*, eds. N. Bednarz, C. Kieran, and L. Lee, 87–106. Dordrecht, the Netherlands: Kluwer.

Leitzel, J. 1989. "Critical Considerations for the Future of Algebra Instruction." In *Research Issues in the Learning and Teaching of Algebra*, eds. S. Wagner and C. Kieran, 27–32. Reston, VA: National Council of Teachers of Mathematics.

Lodholz, R. 1990. "The Transition from Arithmetic to Algebra." In *Algebra for Everyone*, ed. E. Edwards, 24–33. Reston, VA: National Council of Teachers of Mathematics.

Ma, L. 1999. *Knowing and Teaching Elementary Mathematics: Teachers' Understanding of Fundamental Mathematics in China and the United States*. Mahwah, NJ: Lawrence Erlbaum.

Mason, J. 1996. "Expressing Generality and Roots of Algebra." In *Approaches to Algebra: Perspectives for Teaching*, eds. N. Bedarz, C. Kieran, and L. Lee, 65–86. Dordrecht, the Netherlands: Kluwer.

Mason, J., L. Burton, and K. Stacey. 1982. *Thinking Mathematically*. London: Addison-Wesley.

McClain, K., and P. Cobb. 2001. "An Analysis of the Development of Sociomathematical Norms in One First-Grade Classroom." *Journal for Research in Mathematics Education* 32 (3): 236–66.

National Council of Teachers of Mathematics (NCTM). 1991. *Professional Standards for Teaching Mathematics*. Reston, VA: NCTM.

———. 2000. *Principles and Standards for School Mathematics*. Reston, VA: NCTM.

Nesher, P. 1987. "Towards an Instructional Theory: The Role of Students' Misconceptions." *For the Learning of Mathematics* 7 (3): 33–39.

Noss, R., L. Healy, and C. Hoyles. 1997. "The Construction of Mathematical Meanings: Connecting the Visual with the Symbolic." *Educational Studies in Mathematics* 33: 203–33.

Orton, A., and L. Frobisher. 1996. *Insights into Teaching Mathematics*. London: Cassell.

Paley, V. 1990. *The Boy Who Would Be a Helicopter: The Uses of Storytelling in the Classroom*. Cambridge: Harvard University Press.

———. 1993. *You Can't Say You Can't Play*. Chicago: University of Chicago Press.

Pegg, J., and E. Redden. 1990. "Procedures for, and Experiences in, Introducing Algebra in New South Wales." *Mathematics Teacher* 83: 386–91.

Pesek, D., and D. Kirschner. 2000. "Interference of Instrumental Instruction in Subsequent Relational Learning." In *Lessons Learned from Research*, eds. J. Sowder and B. Schappelle, 101–7. Reston, VA: National Council of Teachers of Mathematics.

RAND, M. S. P. 2002. *Mathematical Proficiency for All Students: Toward a Strategic Research and Development Program in Mathematics Education* (DRU-2773-OERI). Arlington, VA: RAND Education and Science and Technology Policy Institute.

Ritchhart, R. 1997. "Exploring Functional Relationships." In *Through Mathematical Eyes: Exploring Functional Relationships in Math and Science*, ed. R. Ritchhart, 9–23. Portsmouth, NH: Heinemann.

Rutherford, F. J. 1997. "Thinking Quantitatively About Science." In *Why Numbers Count: Quantitative Literacy for Tomorrow's America*, ed. L. A. Steen, 60–74. New York: The College Board.

Sawyer, W. W. Quoted in M. Burns, "Arithmetic: The Last Holdout." *Phi Delta Kappan*. February, 1994, 476.

Schoenfeld, A. H. 1985. *Mathematical Problem-Solving*. New York: Academic.

———. 1988. "When Good Teaching Leads to Bad Results: The Disasters of 'Well-Taught' Mathematics Courses." *Educational Psychologist* 23 (2): 145–66.

Schoenfeld, A., and A. Arcavi. 1988. "On the Meaning of Variable." *Mathematics Teacher* 81: 420–27.

Shulman, L. 1987. "Knowledge and Teaching Foundations of the New Reform." *Harvard Educational Review* 57 (1): 1–22.

Schwab, J. J. 1969. *College Curriculum and Student Protest*. Chicago: University of Chicago Press.

Schwartz, D. 1999. "The Productive Agency That Drives Collaborative Learning." In *Collaborative Learning: Cognitive and Computational Approaches*, ed. P. Dillenbourg, 197–241. New York: Pergamon.

Schwartz, D., and J. Bransford. 1998. "A Time for Telling." *Cognition and Instruction* 16 (4): 475–522.

Sherin, M. 2002. "A Balancing Act: Developing a Discourse Community in a Mathematics Classroom." *Journal of Mathematics Teacher Education* 5: 205–33.

Sherin, M. G., D. A. Louis, and E. P. Mendez. 2000. "Students' Building on Each Other's Mathematical Ideas." *Mathematics Teaching in the Middle School* 6 (3): 122–25.

Shulman, J. H. 1992. "Teacher-Written Cases with Commentaries: A Teacher-Researcher Collaboration." In *Case Methods in Teacher Education*, ed. J. H. Shulman, 131–54. New York: Teachers College Press.

Shulman, L. 1986. "Those Who Understand: Knowledge Growth in Teaching." *Educational Researcher* (February): 4–14.

———. 1992. "Toward a Pedagogy of Cases." In *Case Methods in Teacher Education*, ed. J. H. Shulman, 1–32. New York: Teachers College Press.

Silver, E. A. 1994. "On Mathematical Problem Posing." *For the Learning of Mathematics* 14 (1): 19–28.

———. 1997. "'Algebra for All': Increasing Students' Access to Algebraic Ideas, Not Just Algebra Courses." *Mathematics Teaching in the Middle School* 2 (4): 204–7.

Skemp, R. 1978. "Relational Understanding and Instrumental Understanding." *Arithmetic Teacher* 26: 9–15.

Stacey, K., and M. MacGregor. 1997. "Ideas About Symbolism That Students Bring to Algebra." *Mathematics Teacher* 90 (2): 111–13.

Staples, M. 2004. *Developing a Community of Collaborative Learners: Reconfiguring Roles, Relationships and Practices in a High School Mathematics Class*. Stanford, CA: Stanford University.

Steen, L. 1990. "Pattern." In *On the Shoulders of Giants*, ed. L. Steen, 1–10. Washington, DC: National Academy Press.

———. 1997. *Why Numbers Count: Quantitative Literacy for Tomorrow's America*. New York: College Entrance Examination Board.

Stein, M. K., M. Smith, M. Henningsen, and E. Silver. 2000. *Implementing Standards Based Mathematics Instruction: A Case Book for Professional Development*. New York: Teachers College Press.

Thomson, A. G., R. A. Philipp, P. W. Thompson, and B. Boyd. 1994. "Calculational and Conceptual Orientations in Teaching Mathematics." In *Professional Development for Teachers of Mathematics: 1994 Yearbook*, eds. D. Aichele and A. Coxford, 79–91. Reston, VA: National Council of Teachers of Mathematics.

Thornton, S. 2001. "New Approaches to Algebra: Have We Missed the Point?" *Mathematics Teaching in the Middle School* 6 (7): 388–92.

Thorpe, J. 1989. "Algebra: What Should We Teach and How Should We Teach It?" In *Research Issues in the Learning and Teaching of Algebra*, eds. S. Wagner and C. Kieran, 11–24. Reston, VA: National Council of Teachers of Mathematics.

Van Dyke, F., and T. Craine. 1997. "Equivalent Representations in the Learning of Algebra." *Mathematics Teacher* 90 (8): 616–19.

Wagner, S. 1983. "What Are These Things Called Variables?" *Mathematics Teacher* 76, 474–79.

Wagner, S., and C. Kieran. 1989. "An Agenda for Research on the Learning and Teaching of Algebra." In *Research Issues in the Teaching and Learning of Algebra*, 220–37. Reston, VA: National Council of Teachers of Mathematics.

Wagner, S., and S. Parker. 1993. "Advancing Algebra." In *Research Ideas for the Classroom: High School Mathematics*, 119–39. New York: Macmillan.

Warrington, M. 1997. "How Children Think About Division with Fractions." *Mathematics Teaching in the Middle School* 2 (6): 390–94.

Wentzel, K. R. 1997. "Student Motivation in Middle School: The Role of Perceived Pedagogical Caring." *Journal of Educational Psychology* 90: 202–9.

Wheeler, D. 1996. "Rough or Smooth? The Transition from Arithmetic to Algebra in Problem Solving." In *Approaches to Algebra: Perspectives for Teaching*, eds. N. Bednarz, C. Kieran, and L. Lee, 147–49. Dordrecht, The Netherlands: Kluwer.

Wertheim, M. 1997. *Pythagoras' Trousers: God, Physics and the Gender Wars.* New York: W. W. Norton and Company.

White, B., and J. Frederiksen. 1998. "Inquiry, Modeling and Metacognition: Making Science Accessible to All Students." *Cognition and Instruction* 16 (1): 3–118.

Wilson, S. M. 1992. "A Case Concerning Content: Using Case Studies to Teach About Subject Matter." In *Case Methods in Teacher Education*, ed. J. H. Shulman, 64–89. New York: Teachers College Press.

Yackel, E., and P. Cobb. 1996. "Sociomathematical Norms, Argumentation, and Autonomy in Mathematics." *Journal for Research in Mathematics Education* 27 (4): 458–77.